18

THE OPEN MEDIA PAMPHLET SERIES

Cutting Corporate Welfare

RALPH NADER

Foreword by Winona LaDuke

SEVEN STORIES PRESS / New York

Copyright © 2000 by Ralph Nader
Foreword © 2000 by Winona LaDuke

A Seven Stories Press First Edition
Open Media Pamphlet Series editor Greg Ruggiero.

Seven Stories Press, 140 Watts Street, New York, NY 10013;
www.sevenstories.com and www. sevenstories.com/textbook

In Canada:
Hushion House, 36 Northline Road, Toronto, Ontario M4B 3E2

In the U.K.:
Turnaround Publisher Services Ltd., Unit 3, Olympia Trading Estate,
Coburg Road, Wood Green, London N22 6TZ

In Australia:
Tower Books, 9/19 Rodborough Road, Frenchs Forest NSW 2086

Library of Congress Cataloging-in-Publication Data
Nader, Ralph.
    Cutting corporate welfare / Ralph Nader.—Seven Stories Press 1st ed.
    p.   cm. — (Open media pamphlet series; 18)
ISBN 158322-033-X (pbk.)
1. Subsidies—United States. I. Title. II. Series.
HC110.S9 N33 2000
338.973'02—dc21   00-020219

College professors may order examination copies of Seven Stories Press
titles for a free six-month trial period. To order, visit www.sevensto-
ries.com/textbook, or fax on school letterhead to (212) 226-1411.

Book design by Cindy LaBreacht
9 8 7 6 5 4 3 2 1
Printed in the U.S.A.

CONTENTS

FOREWORD by Winona LaDuke

"Who gave them these rights? Why do their rights supercede mine?"—Loretta Pascal, Lil'wat First Nation, in questioning the rights of logging companies to devastate her land, 1995

Pascal's question is as contemporary as it is generations old: Why should the richest interests in the world have "special rights" and entitlements that ordinary citizens do not? It's the question that recently drove thousands into the streets of Seattle and Washington, D.C., and the question that has driven the indigenous communities of Mexico into rebellion since January 1994. For the past forty years, Ralph Nader has also asked this question. He has asked it with his writings, and he has asked it with his actions. In this pamphlet, Nader continues to ask this same question. He answers by directly confronting the U.S. government's practice of subsidizing big business, and by pushing for new laws that would protect from corporate intrusion the personal lives of the vast majority of people who do not have the budget to hire lobbyists to privilege their interests inside the beltway.

In *Cutting Corporate Welfare*, Nader reveals just how deeply private corporations have been drawing from the public trough, and the modus operandi of their practices. Nader describes how corporations siphon from our collective wealth—the federal budget and many state and county assets—while surveying the "frontiers" that they have yet to fully plunder, such as schools parks, the oceans, the Amazon, space, the wind, cyberspace, public attention and the federal budget.

Nader illustrates that it is not the mysterious hand of Adam Smith, or some sort of social Darwinism that permits corporate interests and the super-rich to appropriate public resources, but instead a series of misapplied laws and policies that uphold the centuries-old practice of concentrating wealth in the hands of a few. And, as Nader points out, it is in our power to change these laws.

From the first "explorers" who appropriated land for Christian kingdoms and a Christian God, to the antiquated 1872 Mining Act, laws and policies have been imposed to institutionalize private concentration of power. The Dutch West Indian Trading Company, the Northwest Company, and the Hudson Bay Company were just a few of the many early corporations that set out to make a fortune by institutionalizing unjust practices and laws. The dominance of these early trading companies in the "New World" continued for many generations, and included practices of economic destabilization, land appropriation, genocide, and drug dealing, that were supported by the colonial governments at the time. These corporations provided the financial footholds for some major monied interests today, and, in the case of the Hudson Bay Company, continue to this day as a primary economic power in many communities in northern Canada.

In 1862, then-President Lincoln made deals in the American west that opened up vast areas of Native lands to American settlers. It was the cattle barons who clearly benefited the most. With the passage of the Taylor Grazing Act, the cattle barons' interests were scripted into public policy. Today, the legacy is painful: more than 270 million acres of "public lands" are used primarily by cattle ranchers at bargain basement prices—$1.80 a month, or around $35 million total—for use of those millions of acres. The private appropriation of public lands has led to a very privileged life for some, and massive loss for the rest of us.

That legacy continued when two years later, in 1864, Congress created the North Pacific Railroad Company and ordained that it should construct a railway from Lake Superior to Puget Sound. Along with this proclamation, Congress granted the North Pacific around 40 million acres of land, or 2 percent of the continent, which at the time was Native land. Today, we see the painful legacy of these holdings. Corporate descendants of the North Pacific Railroad—Burlington Northern (the largest), and its associates Weyerhauser, Potlatch, Boise Cascade; and others—continue to clearcut vast areas of forested land, creating a patchwork of destabilized, traumatized ecosystems.

Is this democracy? No, but as Ralph Nader shows, it is through democracy that we can fight back. First with information, then with action.

Here, Ralph Nader presents the information. He offers a concise and cut-to-the-quick analysis that takes the mask off of corporate welfare, and allows us to see the outmoded public policies for what they are—involuntary gifts from all of us to the rich. Based on testimony Nader gave to Congress, *Cutting Corporate Welfare* is a superb analysis and indictment of corporate power; it provides all of us with a tool to challenge the intrusion of these corporations into our lives, our ecosystems, and our economies.

CUTTING CORPORATE WELFARE

INTRODUCTION

Corporate welfare—the enormous and myriad subsidies, bailouts, giveaways, tax loopholes, debt revocations, loan guarantees, discounted insurance and other benefits conferred by government on business—is a function of political corruption. Corporate welfare programs siphon funds from appropriate public investments, subsidize companies ripping minerals from federal lands, enable pharmaceutical companies to gouge consumers, perpetuate anti-competitive oligopolistic markets, injure our national security, and weaken our democracy.

At a time when the national GDP is soaring, one in five children lives in deep poverty, one might expect that a public effort to curtail welfare would focus on cutting big handouts to rich corporations, not small supports for poor individuals. But somehow the invocations of the need for stand-on-your-own-two-feet responsibility do not apply to large corporations.

At a time when even growing federal budget surpluses do not persuade our nation's political leaders to devote public resources to repairing and enhancing the built elements of our commonwealth—such as the nation's schools, bridges, clinics, roads, drinking water systems, courthouses, public transportation systems, and water treatment facilities—one might expect to see calls to divert taxpayer monies from flowing into private corporate hands and instead direct them to crying public needs. But somehow the cramped federal budget—as well as similarly situated state and local budgets—always has room for another corporate welfare program.

This is a deeply rooted problem, one which cuts across party lines. Democrats and Republicans are both culpable for the proliferation of corporate welfare spending. Indeed, the leading Congressional crusader against corporate welfare has long been outgoing House Budget Committee Chair John Kasich, R-Ohio, and efforts to forge bipartisan coalitions to take on corporate welfare founder more on lack of Democratic support than Republican.

Patching the corporate drain on public resources will require an informed and mobilized citizenry that both forces changes in our systems of campaign finance, lobbying and political influence, and demands careful and critical scrutiny by the media, Congressional committees, and ultimately the citizens who lose out from government transfers of resources, privileges, and immunities to corporations.

This pamphlet is part of such an effort to inform, arouse, and mobilize to change the corporate welfare state.

THE POLITICAL ORIGINS OF CORPORATE WELFARE

It is raw political power that creates and perpetuates most corporate welfare programs. There is no serious public policy argument for why television broadcasters should be given control of the digital television spectrum—a $70 billion asset—for free. The endless tax loopholes that riddle the tax code—such as an accelerated depreciation schedule that's worth billions to oil companies—cannot be explained by any exotic theory of fair taxation. Local taxpayers rather than billionaire team owners pay for the new sports stadiums and arenas that dot the American landscape because of the political leverage sports teams and their allies gain through corporate cash and the threat to move elsewhere.

An examination of corporate welfare is, therefore, at one important level, an examination of the state of our political democracy. Unfortunately, the burgeoning corporate welfare state does not speak well for the state of democratic affairs. The following examples, discussed in more detail later in this pamphlet, illustrate how political payoffs—what former Member of Congress Cecil Heftel, D-Hawaii, calls "legalized bribery"—distort decision-making so that the public commonwealth is corporatized to enrich the already-rich.

The savings and loan debacle. Perhaps still the largest corporate welfare expenditure of all time—ultimately set to cost taxpayers $500 billion in principal and interest—the S&L bailout is in large part a story of political corruption, the handiwork of the industry's legion of lobbyists and political payoffs to campaign contributors. The well-connected S&L industry successfully lobbied Congress for a deregulatory bill in the early 1980s, which freed the industry from historic constraints and paved the way for the speculative and corrupt failures that came soon after. Then more industry campaign contributions and lobbying led the Congress to delay addressing the problem—

resulting in more S&L failures and skyrocketing costs for corrective measures. When Congress finally did address the problem, it put the bailout burden—totaling hundreds of billions of dollars—on the backs of taxpayers, rather than on the financial industry.

The costs of S&L deregulation and the subsequent bailout were, and remain, severe both in monetary terms and in the mutation and eventual destruction of an industry that contributed to broader home ownership among all Americans. "In the end," writes economics commentator William Greider, "the goal of housing was thrown over the side and the government's regulatory system was perversely diverted to a different purpose— "socializing" the losses accumulated by freewheeling bankers and developers by making every taxpayer pay for them." Congress even refused in the bailout legislation to include measures to empower consumers to band together into financial consumer associations—a modest quid pro quo that would have imposed zero financial cost on taxpayers or financial institutions and that would have enabled consumers to act on their own to prevent *future* S&L-style crises and bailouts.[1]

Of the many factors contributing to the S&L debacle, which festered throughout the 1980s and into the early 1990s, none was more important than industry lobbying money and campaign cash. "Leaving aside the financial and economic complexities," writes economics commentator William Greider, "the savings and loan bailout is most disturbing as a story of politics—a grotesque case study of how representative democracy has been deformed."[2]

"At every turn, any effort to rein in the thrifts' powers and accountability has been shackled," Representative

Jim Leach, R-Iowa, then a House Banking Committee member and now the Committee chair, told the *Los Angeles Times* in 1989. "If there ever has been a case for campaign finance reform, this is it."[3]

The giveaway of the digital television spectrum. In 1996, Congress quietly handed over to existing broadcasters the rights to broadcast digital television on the public airwaves—a conveyance worth $70 billion—in exchange for... nothing.

Although the public owns the airwaves, the broadcasters have never paid for the rights to use them. New digital technologies now make possible the broadcast of digital television programming (the equivalent of the switch from analog records to digitized compact disks), and the broadcasters sought rights to new portions of the airwaves. In recent years, the Federal Communications Commission has, properly, begun to recognize the large monetary value of the licenses it conveys to use the public airwaves—including for cell phones, beepers, and similar uses—and typically auctions licenses. The 1996 Telecommunications Act, however, prohibited such an auction for distribution of digital television licenses, the most valuable of public airwave properties, and mandated that they be given to existing broadcasters.

How to explain this giveaway, especially when other industries, such as data transmission companies, were eager to bid for the right to use the spectrum?

Look no further than the National Association of Broadcasters (NAB).

The broadcasters are huge political donors, donating about $3 million in the 1995-1996 election cycle. They have close ties to key political figures, most notably

Senate Majority Leader Trent Lott, R-Mississippi; NAB head Eddie Fritts is Lott's college friend. Lott took good care of his buddy, threatening the FCC in no uncertain terms if it failed to promptly oversee the transfer of the licenses to the broadcasters.

Above all, the broadcasters are able to leverage their control over the most important media into influence over politicians. Not surprisingly, the nightly news was silent on this giant giveaway. Few if any Members of Congress were willing to challenge the giveaway. Most feared that bucking the industry would result in slanted news coverage in the next election. Those few who feel secure in their position figure it is not worth taking on the broadcasters—given the fealty of their fellow Members to the industry; they conclude, why bother?

And again, the giveaway not only represents the failure of our working democracy, but an additional erosion. Congress and the FCC failed to include provisions in the legislative and regulatory allocation of the spectrum to force the broadcasters to serve the public interest in concrete ways—for example, by providing free air time for political candidates, or by ceding partial control of the airwaves to citizen groups to air civic programming. (A vague public interest obligation imposed on the broadcasters remains without concrete definition, but preliminary efforts to specify those obligations are underwhelming.)

The 1872 Mining Act. This nearly 130-year-old relic of efforts to settle the West allows mining companies to claim federal lands for $5 an acre or less and then take gold, silver, lead or other hard-rock minerals with no royalty payments to the public treasury. Thanks to the anachronistic 1872 Mining Act, mining companies—including foreign companies—extract billions of dollars worth of minerals a year from federal lands, royalty free.

Legislative efforts to repeal or reform the mining give-away regularly fail, blocked by senators from western states. These senators are *not* standing up for their states' best economic interests; the giveaway mines create few jobs and massive environmental problems with high economic costs in foregone tourist and recreational revenues and uses. The senators *are* standing up for the mine companies, which pour millions in campaign contributions into the Congress.

From 1987 to 1994, the mining companies gave $17 million in campaign contributions to congressional candidates—a small price to pay to preserve their right to extract $26 billion worth of minerals, royalty free, during the same period.[4] More recently, in the 1997-1998 election cycle, the industry—led by the National Mining Association, Cyprus Amax Minerals, Drummond, Phelps Dodge and Peabody Coal—rained more than $2 million in contributions on congressional candidates.[5]

Those campaign donations are concentrated on a relatively small number of key members who go to bat for the industry—including Senators Larry Craig, R-Idaho, and Pete Domenici, R-New Mexico, and Representatives J.D. Hayworth, R-Arizona, and Don Young, D-Alaska. Because of the way the Congress, especially the Senate, functions, it is much easier to block changes in the status quo than to enact changes. The industry's focused contributions ensures it has enough heavyweights and devotees on call in the Congress to block the perennial efforts to reform the 1872 Mining Act.

The mining industry, along with other resource extractive industries, has helped create and fund a front group, People for the West!, that claims to represent the interests of western state citizens but somehow always manages to lobby for corporate positions—such as maintenance of the Mining Act.

Tax loopholes and subsidies. If anyone needs convincing about the need for campaign finance and political reform, they need look no further than the Internal Revenue Code.

The Code is riddled with calculated loopholes, exemptions, credits, accelerated depreciation schedules, deductions and targeted exceptions—many of unfathomable consequence even to trained experts—that are carefully crafted to benefit one or a handful of companies and exist solely because well-paid lobbyists representing fat cat campaign contributors managed to convince a legislator to insert a special provision in long, complicated tax bills.

The origin of many of the corporate tax loopholes is the stuff of Washington legend. It represents one of the worst distortions of our political democracy. Well-heeled lobbyists, who spin through the revolving door between government and K Street and represent high-donor corporate interests, facilitate backroom deals that save their clients millions (or billions). The taxpayers, of course, lose commensurate amounts.

To take one recent egregious example, a conference committee, reportedly acting in response to instructions from then-Speaker Newt Gingrich and Senate Majority Leader Trent Lott, inserted a tax break—not included in the previous House or Senate versions—in the 1997 tax bill that provided special benefits for Amway Corporation and a few others. The tax break came a few months after Amway founder Richard De Vos and his wife Helen

De Vos each gave half million dollar soft money contributions to the Republican National Committee. The revision to Internal Revenue Code Section 1123 applies to two Amway affiliates and four other companies, and will cost taxpayers $19 million over 10 years, according to the Joint Committee on Taxation.[6]

Another extraordinary example occurred the same year. In July 1997, the House and Senate Republican leadership, with the apparent awareness of the Clinton White House, slipped a one-sentence provision into the tax bill that would have saved the tobacco industry $50 billion on the money it was expected to pay as part of a federally approved settlement of the state's lawsuits against the industry. Once the provision was publicly disclosed, many Members of Congress claimed not to have known it was included in the complicated tax bill. Revealed in the light of day, this massive tax favor for an industry falling rapidly out of political favor quickly withered. Both Congressional chambers soon voted to repeal the tobacco industry tax credit—a sign that, despite the fundamental flaws in the political system, news coverage and public outrage can still thwart corporate efforts to loot the treasury.[7]

Pentagon merger subsidies. No government agency is cozier with industry than the Department of Defense, and corporate welfare is pervasive at the agency famous for cost-overruns, waste, fraud, and abuse. Among the most galling of Defense Department corporate welfare handouts is the Pentagon's merger subsidy program, which pays defense contractors to merge, lessening competition for government bids and increasing the lobbying power of newly combined defense megafirms.

The Pentagon subsidy plan began in the early and mid 1990s, when it decided to encourage consolidation in the defense sector. The industry asked for and won encouragement in the form of payments to cover the costs of consolidation—including extravagant "golden parachute" bonuses to executives of acquired companies.

When Lockheed merged with Martin Marietta, taxpayers paid for $30 million in bonuses for company executives—an outrage that Representative Bernie Sanders, the independent from Vermont, finally ended with a legislative amendment barring future "payoffs for layoffs."

Levels of industry concentration in the defense sector are now so high that the antitrust authorities are beginning to intervene to block some new mergers among primary contractors. But other defense mergers continue to proceed—with the help of the U.S. taxpayer.

Hijacking local democracy. Perhaps nothing illustrates the ruthlessness and shameless power plays of the corporate welfare kings than their extortionate demands for state and local subsidies on threat of picking up and moving elsewhere.

And no case illustrates the hijacking of democratic procedures more clearly than billionaire Paul Allen's buying of an especially-made-for-Allen Washington state referendum to approve $300 million in public subsidies to build a football stadium for his Seattle Seahawks. Mega-billionaire Allen, co-founder of Microsoft with Bill Gates and one of the richest men in the world, bought the referendum both literally and figuratively.

In a stunningly brazen maneuver, he paid the state of Washington for the costs of running the special referendum election in June 1997. Although later challenged as a violation of the state's constitution, the state Supreme Court upheld the private financing of the election. But even the Supreme Court majority which upheld the constitutionality of the election purchase blanched at its political ramifications. "Troubling questions may arise, such as whether any wealthy entity could persuade the legislature to place a measure on the ballot provided the costs of the election were paid," wrote Justice Barbara Madsen for the majority.[8]

Having paid for the issue to get on the ballot, Allen then waged a $6.3 million campaign—the most expensive in Washington state history—to convince voters to support the $300 million public subsidy to the stadium. He devoted $2.3 million to radio and TV ads. In total, Allen outspent opponents of the referendum by a 42-to-1 margin.[9]

Allen's investment proved just enough: Washington voters, initially opposed by overwhelming numbers to the idea of public funding for the stadium, approved the referendum with a 51 percent majority.

DOUBLE STANDARDS FOR THE POOR AND THE POWERFUL

Simply to acknowledge the existence of corporate welfare is to point to the enormous discrepancies in influence and allocation of resources in our country.

While President Clinton and the Congress have gutted the welfare system for poor people—fulfilling a pledge to "end welfare as we know it"—no such top-down agenda has emerged for corporate welfare recipients. The savage demagoguery directed against imaginary "welfare queens" has never been matched with parallel denunciations of gluttonous corporate welfare kings—the DuPonts, General Motors and Bristol-Myers-Squibbs that embellish their palaces with riches taken from the public purse.

While the minimal government benefits still afforded the poor are provided only to the most impoverished, no such "means testing" is applied to corporate welfare beneficiaries. By and large, the bigger the company, the more it extracts in government supports. The many government programs to benefit small business—some merited, some not—do not come close to the subsidies lavished on large multinational corporations. When Daimler-Chrysler threatens to move a factory expansion out of the city of Toledo unless the city effectively evicts an entire neighborhood, turns the land over to the automaker, and arranges hundreds of millions in federal, state and local tax benefits and other subsidies, Toledo rushes to comply. If "Joe's Garage" were to make such demands, the city would laugh. (In fact, in Toledo's desperate rush to please DaimlerChrysler, the city has undertaken what appears to be a campaign of harassment and intimidation designed to push a local auto body repair shop—Kim's Auto Body—out of business, and out of the way of DaimlerChrysler's plans to expand its grounds. Note the word choice: those are plans to expand the *grounds*, not the factory. Kim's and the surrounding neighborhood is located not where factory construction will take place, but where Chrysler would like to place shrubbery.)

The new welfare law sets strict time limits for how long poor people can receive government supports, but no such time limitations attach to government handouts to big business. When it comes to the myriad federal government subsidies, even the names of the beneficiaries are often unknown and almost never centrally compiled for the public, the media, or even government officials. Tax loopholes and tax subsidies generally renew themselves automatically, meaning corporations can take advantage of them into perpetuity (or at least until there is a periodic revamping of the entire tax code, and even such revisions of the tax code usually leave key loopholes in place), without the loophole ever being reexamined. While there are detailed reporting requirements for what remains of welfare for the poor, when it comes to corporate welfare, there are few organized, regular, and current reporting requirements and data compilations, easily accessible by the public.

The welfare law denies benefits even to legal immigrants in this country; corporate welfare, by contrast, is far more non-discriminating—Uncle Sam subsidizes foreign corporations as well as domestic businesses. Can you imagine the Congress deciding to extend the welfare for people program to cover poor Canadians? Maybe not, but the federal government provides millions of dollars in subsidies to Canadian mining companies every year. Tax loopholes enable foreign multinationals doing business in the United States to pay proportionally less than their U.S. counterparts. Chrysler has become Daimler-Chrysler, with its headquarters, top executives and annual shareholder meetings in Germany, yet there is no abatement in Uncle Sam's corporate welfare payments to the company that in 1979 was saved from bankruptcy and collapse by a U.S. taxpayer bailout.

SOCIAL NEEDS SHUNTED ASIDE FOR CORPORATE GREED

Implicit in the juxtaposition of corporate welfare and welfare for poor people is the opportunity cost of subsidies for big business: government money wasted on Ford, Chevron, and Con Ed is not available to meet pressing national needs.

To focus on one critical area, at no time in recent history have we more needed a program to construct, rebuild, or repair crumbling bridges, schools, drinking water facilities, sewer lines, docks, parks, mass transit systems, libraries, clinics, courthouses, and other public amenities and infrastructure. Too many of our roads and bridges are decrepit, school roofs across the nation are leaking or falling in, the public water system does not deliver safe drinking water for millions, the reach of public transportation systems is dwindling, even the great national park system is decaying.

Consider the following sampling:

➤A prerequisite to any serious effort to educate the country's children to be creative, inventive, and dynamic workers, entrepreneurs, consumers, and citizens is providing them with functioning physical facilities, but one in three schools across the United States is "in need of extensive repair or replacement," according to a 1995 General Accounting Office report. Fixing the schools, the GAO estimates, will cost $113 billion over three years.

➤The Centers for Disease Control estimates one million people become sick every year from bad water, with about 900 deaths occurring. The EPA estimates nearly $140 billion will be needed over the next 20 years for water system investments to install, upgrade, or replace failing drinking water infrastructure.

➤Maintaining the public transit system at current levels, the Department of Transportation estimates, will cost $9.7 billion a year. Improving the infrastructure to a condition of "good" would require upping annual expenditures to $14.2 billion a year. However, maintaining or slightly upgrading the public transit is not nearly enough. We need to restore the many large urban public transit systems that were bought and dismantled by a GM-led conspiracy (resulting in a 1949 federal antitrust conviction) earlier this century, and then move beyond. Bold new investments are needed to create a modern mass transit system conducive to livable cities, one which brings community residents closer together, combats the momentum towards sprawl, guarantees lower-income groups the ability to travel efficiently in metropolitan areas, abates air pollution, and improves transportation safety.

►As a society we have failed to respect the foresight of Theodore Roosevelt, John Muir, and the other conservationist founders of the national park system, neglecting to invest sufficient resources to maintain, let alone properly expand, the parks. A Park Service—estimated funding gap of nearly $9 billion has left animal populations at risk, park amenities in substandard or unusable conditions and many national historical artifacts in danger of being lost to posterity.

The hideous disparities between taxpayer subsidies showered on corporate behemoths and unmet social needs are highlighted most clearly in state and local cases, where the revenue and expenditure pools are less complicated than at the federal level.

Consider the case of Cleveland, Ohio. The city has earned renown for a downtown featuring two new publicly financed stadiums, a publicly financed sports arena, a taxpayer-supported rock-n-roll hall of fame, and glittering new buildings receiving millions in tax abatements that come directly out of the school system's revenue stream. At the same time as the city has doled out millions to developers, almost a quarter of the city's schools are so shoddy they should be replaced rather than repaired, according to an architectural and engineering report commissioned by the city school board.[10] Decaying sewers led to a massive downtown flood in January 2000 after a sewer pipe burst. In 1991, one day after the city approved $300 million in financing for a new baseball stadium and basketball arena, the Cleveland school district announced it was phasing-out scholastic athletics for lack of money to equip students and pay coaches and referees.

What is the conceivable rationale for a corporate welfare profligacy that spends hundreds of millions on luxury-box-equipped, amenity-filled stadiums designed for the comfort of the wealthy spectators while fiscal constraints force the shut down of participatory high school sports activities?

THE CORPORATE WELFARE MENTALITY

Yet another indicator of the perversion of sensible thinking engendered by the corporate welfare lobby is the degree to which corporate welfare has been normalized inside the Beltway in Washington, D.C., in state capitols and in city halls across the country.

Consider the Partnership for a New Generation of Vehicles (PNGV). PNGV is a federal government subsidy program ostensibly designed to speed auto industry production of more fuel efficient cars. Its real-world effect, however, has been to forestall any toughening of federal fuel efficiency standards. It has also vectored research investments to a dirty technology, diesel, and permitted the major U.S. automakers (now including Daimler-Chrysler) to collude on do-nothing "research"—suppressing the competition that might result in genuine innovation and, most importantly, deployment of new technologies.

For the entirety of the Clinton administration, the Big Three automakers have hoodwinked Congress and the executive branch with this program that has not even achieved a functioning prototype. Now, with growing concerns over global warming and rising gas prices, it would seem that patience with the industry scam might run out.

No way. Instead, Vice President Gore has bragged about his involvement with PNGV as a sign of his commitment to the environment. Well-intentioned, environmentally-minded members of Congress are loathe to criticize the program, because the Capitol Hill mindset now conceives a subsidy program to the Big Three as an aggressive environmental program—never mind how the industry has used the program to thwart meaningful regulation of fuel efficiency—and they have trouble imagining alternatives.

A NEW FRAMEWORK FOR ANALYZING CORPORATE WELFARE

One of the purposes of this pamphlet is to break through the corporate welfare mentality and propose new approaches for thinking about corporate welfare.

Rejecting corporate-welfare-think, citizens should ask probing question of government subsidy programs for big business:

➤What rationales do private interests use to secure subsidies from the government, and then to shield them from challenge from both the legislative and judicial branches?

➤How do corporate welfare programs become entrenched and immune to cessation or reform?

➤To what extent do foreign corporations benefit from the expenditure of U.S. taxpayer dollars on corporate welfare?

➤How can fair pricing mechanisms be used to allow beneficial programs to be preserved, while eliminating welfare subsidy components?

➤What criteria should be used to determine when corporate welfare programs should simply be cancelled, and when they should be restructured to extract public benefits, pay-backs, or investment returns from the government-supported enterprise?

➤What administrative due process should apply to corporate welfare? How can taxpayers be given standing and procedural rights under the Administrative Procedures Act and other relevant statutes to challenge arbitrary agency action in the corporate welfare area?

➤How do economic subsidies disadvantage non-subsidized competing businesses who pay their dues and foster undesirable market outcomes?

Thinking critically about corporate welfare first requires arriving at a working definition of the term.

Many have offered a working definition that looks to the benefits conferred and costs incurred by a particular program, subsidy, or loophole. According to these definitions, a program is considered corporate welfare if its public cost outweighs its public benefits. Others have asked whether the private, corporate benefit outweighs the overall public benefit. These are important questions—questions which should be asked of any corporate welfare program—but they are too narrow to serve as the basis for defining corporate welfare. Defining corporate welfare in this fashion also immediately orients the debate about any particular program into a contest over the program's merits, with defenders of the program inevitably explaining how it creates jobs and therefore is worthy of taxpayer support.

A more robust definition of corporate welfare looks not to the benefits conferred on the public, but to the benefits conferred on corporations as compared to any corporate payment, or goods or services provided, to the government. If a program involves the government giving more to private companies than it gets back—that is, where it is engaging in a transaction that cannot be justified as a fair market value exchange—then it should be considered corporate welfare. No definition of corporate welfare will be all-inclusive—some element of know-it-when-I-see-it will have to remain, including for pork-laden contracts for unnecessary goods or services— but applied flexibly, this definition serves relatively well.

The advantage of this definition is that it suggests analytic inquiries other than whether a program is "good" or "bad." It allows for the possibility of "good" corporate welfare—programs that confer subsidies on business but are merited because of the overall public gain. (There *are* cases of "good" corporate welfare—but these too should be subjected to proper procedural and substantive checks.)

In deferring the debate over a program's merits, this definition of corporate welfare should channel discussion so that a series of inquisitive screens can be applied to the program, including but not limited to whether the program should be cancelled.

Among the screens that should be applied:

➤Does the program serve some broad public purpose that suggests it has merits beyond the benefits it confers on particular companies? If not, the program should be cancelled.

➤If it does serve some public interest, can the government achieve the same ends or more important public goals by retaining an interest in an asset being given away or doing a service in-house?

➤Does the program involve functions that should properly be left to the market?

➤If the government is going to distribute assets, contracts, or tax breaks to private parties, can and should it do so in a non-exclusive way so that competition is promoted?

➤If the government is going to provide corporations with services, or give away its assets, is there any reason it should not charge, or should charge below-market rates?

➤Are there non-monetary reciprocal obligations that should be demanded of special interests that receive government benefits? These might include, but not be limited to, reasonable pricing of government-subsidized goods and services sold to consumers.

➤Is the program subject to constitutional or other judicial challenge as a waste of taxpayer assets, or use of taxpayer assets for corporate welfare, rather than the general welfare? Does the program exceed an implementing agency's statutory authority? What are the procedural and substantive avenues for citizen challenge of the program to restrain unauthorized agency action?

➤Is there an institutional means of periodic review of the program to ensure it continues to serve its broader public purposes? Are criteria delineated by which the program should be evaluated? Does the program require reauthorization or will it have automatic renewal?

Next, we will categorize the major forms of corporate welfare now in vogue—state and local corporate welfare, government giveaways, government-funded research and development, bailouts, tax expenditures, government-sponsored enterprises, loans and loan guarantees, export and overseas marketing assistance, defense, transportation and other pork, loans and loan guarantees, and grants and direct subsidies—provide illustrative examples of each category, and begin the process of critical scrutiny suggested by the inquisitive screens outlined above.

THE CORPORATE WELFARE STATE

STATE AND LOCAL CORPORATE WELFARE

Large corporations routinely pit states and cities against each other in bidding contests that are structurally biased in favor of Big Business. The price of their doing business, they communicate explicitly and implicitly, is massive subsidization by local and state authorities—through tax abatements, government financing of building projects, improper use of eminent domain, assumption of corporate liabilities, waiver of regulations, or other supports. This is corporate welfare in its rawest form—evidenced by the brazen threats to move, the drain on funding for schools and essential state and local services, the shameless opposition to minimalist requests for reciprocity in the form of job guarantees or payment of living wages to employees.

Although many state and local corporate welfare programs are generic—such as tax increment financing provided to companies locating in a particular geographic area—many tax breaks and abatements are directed to specific companies. They properly raise the public ire—as citizens demand to know why the rich and powerful have taxes forgiven while local small businesses are required to pay their fair share without special dispensation—and should sharpen the cutting edge of a nascent movement to end corporate welfare as we know it.

THE TOLEDO SHAKEDOWN AND EMINENT DOMAIN ABUSE

In Toledo, DaimlerChrysler has brought a frightened and financially strapped city to its knees. Desperate to keep a Jeep plant in the city, Toledo showered a $300 million local, state, and federal subsidy package on the multinational corporation to support company plant expansion plans. The package includes a property exemption for 10 years, transfer of free land, including site preparation, transfer of environmental liability from Daimler-Chrysler to the city, and assorted other handouts. All of this is offered in exchange for a Jeep facilities expansion plan that is expected to result in a reduction of Jeep jobs from the current 5,600 to 4,900 (DaimlerChrysler's public claim) or 4,200 (the level the company specifies it will try to preserve in an unenforceable provision in its agreement with Toledo) or something much lower (a likely result based on United Auto Worker estimates and recent layoffs at the plant).

The Jeep agreement is remarkable, as are many of the special state and local corporate welfare deals, for being so poorly drafted from the city's point of view, so one-sided and tilted in favor of the corporate beneficiary. There is virtually no binding reciprocal obligation on DaimlerChrysler in the agreement—to create jobs, maintain a certain job level, or to agree to set wage levels or working conditions. In exchange for no binding commitments and no share of the profits, Toledo has agreed to put up huge sums of money, much of it borrowed.

The most outrageous element of Toledo's Jeep deal is that it requires the displacement of a community near the plant. As it turns out from DaimlerChrysler's plans, the company does not even genuinely intend to use the land that the city will transfer to it from 83 homeowners. In its public explanations, Jeep identifies the community's parcel as a potential truck waiting area; but in its map, the area is to be used for landscaping—a truck waiting area is designated for another parcel of land.

Threatening community residents that it would condemn the entire neighborhood, the city offered to buy their homes. Residents first learned they would be thrown out of their homes and their neighborhood bulldozed not from city officials, but from the *Blade*, Toledo's daily newspaper. The low-ball efforts likely violated the federal Uniform Relocation Act, which requires compensation sufficient to enable displaced people to buy comparable homes or establish businesses in similar or better neighborhoods. Many Toledo residents accepted the city's low-ball offer, others held out for somewhat better deals. A handful have resisted.

This fiasco replicates Detroit and GM's shameful collaboration in 1980, when the city used eminent domain to eradicate Poletown, a stable community of 400 homeowners, twelve churches and dozens of small businesses, schools and a hospital. In the Poletown case, GM ultimately built a Cadillac factory which created far fewer jobs than advertised and did not require the destruction of many of the homes.

Indeed, the Toledo-DaimlerChrysler eminent domain scheme marks what is a growing corporate welfare trend whereby states and localities abuse their eminent domain powers to serve private parties.[11] These are many of the most heart-wrenching instances of corporate welfare, because they often involve the literal destruction of longstanding homes, neighborhoods, and communities. This newly emerging trend echoes the shameful corporate welfare history of ruthless use in the 1950s and 1960s of condemnation powers to uproot inner city communities and transfer valuable property to commercial and real estate developers.

CORPORATE BLACKMAIL AND THE MARRIOTT-MARYLAND CASE

While the implied threat of DaimlerChrysler moving loomed in the background of the Toledo dispute (city officials admitted fear of the company fleeing motivated their extraordinary generosity), the threat of corporate flight was in the foreground of Marriott's recent, successful effort to blackmail the state of Maryland into providing a $31 million to $47 million subsidy package.

In 1997, the company announced that its Bethesda, Maryland headquarters were no longer large enough to house its expanding workforce of 3,800. It created a search committee to decide where the company's new headquarters should be based. Company CEO Bill Marriott announced that the company would be willing to move to a new state if compelling financial reasons justified it. Virginia leaped into the bidding war. Virginia Governor James Gilmore III and former Governor George Allen both actively attempted to seduce Marriott to step across the border to take advantage of Virginia's lower tax rates.

Faced with Virginia's enticements, and with Marriott's cultivated indecision, Maryland progressively augmented its offer to the company.

When Marriott finally announced its intentions to remain in Maryland, state officials celebrated their victory over their neighbors. "Our team is red-hot, Virginia's team is all shot," Maryland House speaker Casper Taylor, told the *Washington Post*.[12]

But in the bidding war Marriott cultivated between Maryland and Virginia, the only winner was Marriott. The corporate welfare package bestowed on Marriott did absolutely nothing to create new jobs. Marriott had already determined that it would expand its headquarters because of its growth and profitability—and that decision was made without regard to whether it would receive tax breaks in the state where it would base its headquarters.[13]

After the giveaway, William Skiner, president of the Maryland Taxpayers Association, suggested that companies that receive public money should issue stock to state residents. "They have my address. Where are my shares?" he asked.

Of course the answer to that entirely reasonable question is: there are none.

Nor are there similar subsidies available to small businesses. They do not have the political clout, nor the plausible threat to move out of state, to leverage comparable corporate welfare packages. This imbalance creates a very real competitive , and local services as a 20-room inn or other small business, but do not pay a proportionate share of the taxes that fund these services.

After the tax subsidy deal was completed, the *Baltimore Sun* reported that Marriott had decided on remaining in Maryland before the state made its last, more generous offer.[14] According to the *Sun's* report, Virginia officials were aware of the Marriott decision, but remained silent—enabling the company to extract more money from the state of Maryland.

PLAYING FOR ALL THE MONEY: STADIUMS, GAMBLING, AND CORPORATE WELFARE

Among the most outrageous types of bidding for business involves sports stadiums. The pattern is now familiar:[15] the local sports team, owned by a megamillionaire in virtually every case except for the publicly owned Green Bay Packers football team, threatens to move unless the city bestows a glamorous, and extraordinarily expensive, publicly financed new stadium on the team. Inevitably, the stadium is required to contain luxury boxes and high-priced seats which help fill the teams coffers, but put watching the local team out of reach for significant portions of the town's population. If the city refuses to capitulate to the team's demands, the team, especially if it is a football team, typically follows through on its threat, and moves to a new location.

That creates a lose-lose situation for the city: either lose the team, or spend hundreds of millions of dollars for a public facility that will be used entirely or primarily to support a private sports team. Most, but not all, cities choose to subsidize the team, even in the many cases where scholastic athletics, not to mention the schools themselves, are massively underfunded.

Cities that have capitulated to this kind of sports mogul blackmail include Baltimore, Cleveland, Denver, San Diego, Nashville, Indianapolis, Pittsburgh, Miami, San Francisco, St. Louis, Seattle, and Detroit.

Now gambling casinos are looking for similar subsidies. In Detroit, after the city decided to give three giant corporate casino companies an effective license to tax *gambling is voluntary*

~~lower-income people~~ by running casinos, it decided to sweeten the offer further by providing $50 million in development funding and using eminent domain to take prime locations for the gambling houses.

In Atlantic City, the state of New Jersey is contributing more than $200 million in taxpayer dollars for a road-tunnel project and more than 100 acres of free land to entice Steve Wynn's Mirage Resorts to build yet another casino in the city. Building Steve Wynn's driveway has required the destruction of nine houses in the city's most prosperous African-American neighborhood.

(Such tax subsidies, incidentally, are not the only corporate welfare now granted to increasingly politically powerful gambling interests. Public Citizen reports that the Senate Majority Leader inserted a provision into the 1998 IRS Reform Bill that permits employers and employees solely in the casino industry to receive 100 percent tax exemptions for employer-provided meals, regardless of whether workers need to eat on the premises to do their jobs properly. This provision is estimated to save the industry approximately $30 million a year.[16])

GIULIANI'S CORPORATE WELFARE SPENDING SPREE

"This is a free-market economy. Welcome to the era after Communism." So said New York City Mayor Rudolph Giuliani in explaining his foiled plans to sell 112 community gardens to private developers—destroying urban green space that helps build community.

But while Mayor Giuliani may be tough on gardeners and poor people who receive welfare, his free-market credentials are sorely lacking. Under his tenure, New York has practiced an unrestrained form of corporate socialism. New York's previous mayors, Ed Koch and David Dinkins, also embarked on the giveaway path, but Mayor Giuliani is blazing new trails, offering subsidies at about twice the rate as Mayor Dinkins.

Take the $900 million package for the New York Stock Exchange, a naked subsidy to the high capitalist temple of free markets that is ostensibly designed to keep it from moving to New Jersey (an unlikely bluff). This deal, which provides for about $200,000 in subsidies for each "retained" job, isn't the only corporate-welfare arrangement the Mayor has struck with a financial exchange. He has bestowed similar gifts on the American Exchange, the Mercantile Exchange and the Coffee, Sugar and Cocoa Exchange.

Mayor Giuliani has also provided deals—including sales-tax exemptions, property-tax abatements and discounted electricity prices—for media corporations. The beneficiaries include ABC, NBC, Ziff-Davis, McGraw-Hill, Reuters, Condé Nast, Time Warner (expected soon), and Rupert Murdoch's News America. The Mayor gave CBS $10 million in tax breaks and subsidies even though it had already committed to stay in the city through 2008.

For his closest corporate friends, one set of tax breaks is not enough. Some large companies that had already received welfare packages were extended new tax breaks and other subsidies. Among the double dippers: Reuters, Condé Nast, Smith Barney, and Bear, Stearns.

If the Mayor had shown even a little of the toughness he displayed to the city's small gardeners, perhaps the corporate socialism reigning in the financial capital of the world might be a bit more restrained.

CORPORATE WELFARE IN THE GUISE OF COMMUNITY DEVELOPMENT

A more regularized and pervasive form of corporate welfare is commonly described as community development
and made available not on a negotiated case-by-case
basis, but to all businesses locating in certain areas or
meeting certain criteria. By providing a variety of local,
state, and federal tax breaks through creative financing
mechanisms (including tax increment financing), city,
state and community development agencies seek to assist
businesses locating in targeted areas. The economic
development agencies administering these programs are,
in many cases, sincerely trying to facilitate community
development, especially in low-income areas. But there
is generally little reciprocal obligation placed upon the
beneficiaries, either to provide certain kinds of jobs, or
jobs at a living wage, for example. There is also serious
reason to question whether some of the investments
would have occurred in the absence of the incentive, or
whether the tax incentives shift some investments from
a nearby area with little net social gain.

The UCLA Center for Labor Research and Education
and the Los Angeles Alliance for a New Economy recently
conducted one of the most comprehensive reviews of a
local community development effort, focused on the Los
Angeles Community Redevelopment Agency.[17] This
project, it would be fair to say, was favorably disposed
to such community development efforts, but was designed
to help direct public expenditures to realize higher returns
in terms of public benefits. Among the project's findings
and recommendations (which apply directly only to the
Los Angeles agency but probably apply widely): large subsidies to retail operations did not pay off; there was an

under-investment in industrial relative to retail development; small neighborhood shopping centers represented a better investment than large retail complexes; and that record keeping on the results of subsidized ventures is inadequate and needs improvement.

ENDING LOCAL AND STATE CORPORATE WELFARE

No category of corporate welfare is more ripe for a citizen movement to restrain government giveaways than local and state subsidies. It is the arena in which organized citizens can most effectively move policy and change outcomes; and its direct impact in stealing from other budgetary items and the identifiability of beneficiaries should exert a galvanizing effect.

In addition to opposing local and state giveaways, such a movement should support a series of corrective policy initiatives.

First, states and localities should follow the Minnesota lead and adopt a policy of annual disclosure of all corporate welfare recipients.

Second, where state and local governments decide that taxpayer support for business is necessary, they should include binding commitments that recipients deliver on job creation and other promises—with "clawback" provisions that require return of tax and other monetary supports if the promises are not kept.

Addressing state and local corporate welfare will obviously require state and local initiatives. But there is an important federal role, as well.

Third, Congress should authorize and encourage states to enter into compacts in which they refuse to enter a race to the bottom against each other in terms of special tax breaks and related benefits.

Fourth, the federal government should levy a surtax on companies receiving state and local tax breaks, at the very least treating the value of the tax breaks as income upon which federal taxes should be paid. Representative David Minge has introduced legislation towards this end.

On the stadium issue in particular, Senator Arlen Specter's proposal to require Major League Baseball and the National Football League to pay half the costs of any new stadium for teams in their leagues represents a useful starting point for determining how to ensure that the private corporate beneficiaries of stadiums pick up at least a significant part of the tab for their construction.

Fifth, Congress should conduct a review of the use of tax-exempt municipal bonds. Their use to fund corporate welfare, private projects, or public projects that will benefit a narrow business interest (classically, a sports team) should be prohibited. (There may also be merit to considering a replacement of the tax exemption with direct federal transfers to state and local governments—according to Citizens for Tax Justice, such a scheme could transfer more money to state and local governments at less federal cost, while eliminating one kind of local and state corporate welfare.)

Finally, there must be court tests of the claim that the provision of tax subsidies and similar incentives distort economic decision-making concerning the location of business activity and therefore constitutes an unconstitutional infringement on Congress's power to regulate interstate commerce, as has been suggested by Northeastern University Law Professor Peter Enrich.[18] Enrich and Toledo lawyer Terry Lodge are pursuing such a court challenge to the Toledo-DaimlerChrysler deal.

The U.S. federal government is quite probably the richest property owner on earth. The government owns vast tracts of land, including oil and mineral riches, forests, thousands of buildings and plants, the public airwaves and much more.

Giveaways of these assets are one of the purest forms of corporate welfare—a something-for-nothing, or something-for-too-little, proposition. The level of public outrage would be high if the government wrote a $70 billion check to the broadcast industry—but that is effectively what happened when the Federal Communications Commission, pursuant to the Telecommunications Act of 1996, handed over the digital television spectrum to existing broadcasters.

The government retains its property as the shared commonwealth of the people of the United States, and there should be a strong presumption against giving it away. Where a reasoned decision is made to distribute some of that wealth to private parties, the government should explore whether it can distribute the public assets in a non-exclusive, public-purpose way, or in a fashion that promotes competition. When public assets are going to be distributed to private parties, the government should generally receive a market-rate purchase or lease price; and where taxpayer assets are to be distributed to a narrow class of beneficiaries, below-market purchase or rental rates should be accepted only in the most compelling of circumstances. Finally, prior to transfer of government property to private parties, the government should consider whether there are non-monetary reciprocal obligations that should be demanded of recipients—these may include everything from binding promises to adhere to higher environmental standards to contributing equipment to support noncommercial television.

DIGITAL SPECTRUM GIVEAWAY

In one of the single biggest giveaways in U.S. corporate welfare history, the Federal Communications Commission (FCC) on April 7, 1997 donated broadcast licenses for digital television to existing broadcasters.

Under the terms of the giveaway, the broadcasters will pay nothing for the exclusive right to use the public airwaves, even though the FCC itself estimated the value of the digital licenses to be worth \$11 billion to \$70 billion.[19]

The giveaway was mandated, in part, by the 1996 Telecommunications Act, which prohibited, under demands by the broadcaster lobby, the FCC from auctioning off the airwaves. The Telecommunications Act also required the FCC, if it decided to allocate the licenses, to give them only to incumbent broadcasters.

The licenses will permit the broadcasters to air programs through digital signals, which offer higher picture quality than currently used analog broadcasting. FCC rules will require broadcasters in the largest cities to air digital programs in the next few years. All of the broadcasters will continue to air analog versions of their programs, at least during a dozen-year transition period.

The new licenses are for the spectrum equivalent of five or six digital television channels. The broadcasters will be able to use the extra channels to air multiple simultaneous programs or, more likely, for other purposes, potentially including data transfer, subscription video, interactive materials, audio signals and other not-yet-developed innovations. In these enterprises, they will compete at advantage with non-corporate-welfare-receiving companies.

The original theory behind granting the broadcasters such wide spectrum space was to permit them to air high-definition television (HDTV). But many broadcasters may choose not to air HDTV, and instead will receive the extra spectrum channel space as a super-windfall—yielding a revenue stream from non-broadcasting uses of the spectrum, in addition to revenues from airing of digital television broadcasts ... all without paying any license fees to the public owner of the airwaves, the federal government.

As former Senate Majority Leader Bob Dole has recognized, there is no conceivable reason why the incumbent broadcasters should have been given exclusive rights to use the airwaves.[20] Other possible television broadcasters should have been given the right to bid for portions of the digital spectrum, and so should have other potential users, such as data transmission companies.

However, These competing business interests' protestations were completely trumped by the power of the National Association of Broadcasters (NAB).

This is the quintessential perversion of democracy: the broadcasters pay nothing to the public for the right to air programming over the public airwaves; then they use the influence they gain over politicians from their use of these public resources to extort still greater subsidies; and all the while they do not allow this subject to be covered on their news programs.

Only a few weeks after consummating their tremendous, the broadcasters expressed sudden concern with the fate of viewers who would be forced, in 12 years time, to buy new televisions if the broadcasters forfeit their analog stations, as currently scheduled. This would indeed be an extraordinary consumer shakedown, but not one that the broadcasters are positioned to challenge in good faith. They are now lobbying to maintain their analog stations—another public resource which they exploit free of charge. The FCC estimates the value of the analog spectrum at as high as $132 billion.[21]

Lost in the giveaway was the opportunity to set aside portions of the broadcast spectrum for public access, educational, and public interest programming.

There remains an opportunity to rectify at least this failure. The FCC licenses to the broadcasters impose an as-yet-unspecified public interest obligation. This could be defined to include public interest and public access programming. As part of their public interest obligations, the broadcasters should be required to allocate a substantial portion of their new spectrum space and time to public access programming, and to fund quality programming. Specially chartered, democratically governed citizen television networks could develop programming, or moderately funded programming opportunities could be allocated to qualifying civic organizations. Such a modest dose of media democracy can only be good for our nation's democracy.[22]

Others have suggested additional requirements that should be imposed on the broadcasters as public interest obligations. People for Better TV, a national coalition including the American Academy of Pediatrics, the Civil Rights Forum on Communications Policy, the Communications Workers of America, the Consumer Federation of America, the league of United Latin American Citizens, the NAACP, the National Council of Churches and the National Organization for Women, is calling for a debate over and analysis of serious proposals to ensure that broadcasters devote meaningful coverage to public affairs, that the broadcasters respect and nurture rather than exploit children, and that measures are taken to promote racial, ethnic, and gender diversity in television programming.[23]

However, as People for Better TV points out, the Gore Commission which was charged with considering how to define the broadcasters' public interest obligations—remember, again, these obligations are the only payment the broadcasters will make for controlling now $200 billion in taxpayer airwaves assets—failed to rise to the occasion. (The *Los Angeles Times* derided the report as a "national scandal."[24]) Moreover, although the print media devoted some attention to the issue, as People for Better TV notes, "Television stations, perhaps fearing regulation, kept the issue off the local and national news. The discussion about how TV stations will (or will not) serve their community is taking place in the same backroom, deal-making, back-slapping environment that always preoccupies official Washington.

"The spectrum giveaway and the secrecy surrounding this important debate are travesties of American democracy," the coalition rightly concludes.

THE 1872 MINING ACT

No discussion of government giveaways can fail to take note of the absurd Mining Act of 1872.[25] Whatever the merits of the Act at the time of passage, when it was intended to help settle the West, it has long been clear that the Act serves an unjustifiable giveaway to narrow corporate interests, including foreign corporations. As Carl Mayer and George Riley note in their history of the 1872 Mining Act, "Many of the deficiencies noted three of four years after the law's passage have been cited repeatedly by committees and legislators during the last century. The critics have focused on four problems: the failure of the law to return appropriate revenue to the treasury; the inability of the federal government to halt fraudulent acquisition of mineral land; the loss of government control of patented land which passes out of public ownership; and the elevation of mining to the highest use of the land."[26] But reform efforts regularly fail, thanks to mining lobby interests—a lobby with power vastly disproportionate to its economic contributions, which are estimated at about one-tenth of one percent of the West's total income.

Many of the mines on federal or patented land are literally billion-dollar giveaways—often to foreign companies.[27] In 1994, American Barrick Corporation, a Canadian company, patented nearly 2,000 acres of public land in Nevada that contained over $10 billion in recoverable gold reserves. Taxpayers received less than $10,000. In 1995, a Danish company patented land in

Idaho containing more than $1 billion in minerals for a price of $275.

The Washington, D.C.-based Mineral Policy Center estimates that mining companies extract $2 billion to $3 billion in minerals from public lands every year—royalty free. From 1872 to 1993, mining companies took more than $230 billion out of the federal lands, royalty free, according to the Mineral Policy Center.[28]

In 1994, Congress imposed a moratorium on patenting, but already processed patents continue to be filed, and mining companies continue to work already claimed lands.

Third World countries routinely strike better deals with mining companies than does the most powerful government on the planet. A mere 8 percent royalty on existing mines would bring $200 million a year into the federal coffers.[29]

The subsidized mines interfere with other economic and non-economic uses and values of public lands. University of Montana Professor Thomas Power has developed cogent arguments that the destruction of the natural environment associated with mining on federal lands imposes real economic costs, absorbed both by the tourism industry and residents whose land values and basic decisions to live in the West are based in part on the high quality living environment of the region.[30] The Mineral Policy Center estimates direct cleanup costs for the more than a half million abandoned mines on federal lands in the $30 billion to $70 billion range.[31]

In March 1999, the Clinton Administration ruled that it would enforce environmental laws that limit the ability of mining companies to dump waste on public lands, and thereby limit the extent to which hardrock mining can be done. The mining industry has set fast to work to repeal this ruling, though so far it has failed. Maybe Members of Congress are beginning to realize that, for more than a century, they have been generous enough to the mining industry.

INTERNET GIVEAWAYS

An evolving giveaway of public assets involves the management of the U.S. government's internet assets. The federal government currently contracts with Network Solutions, Inc. (NSI), to manage certain domain name registrations (including .com, .net, and .org). After entering into the contract in 1993, NSI was later acquired by Science Applications International Corporation (SAIC) for $3.9 million, and subsequently was permitted to charge U.S. consumers wildly excessive fees for registering internet domain names. NSI's monopoly on the .com and other valuable domain names has turned a tiny initial investment into a firm with a market capitalization of $2.5 billion—thanks to control of the power to sell the public the right to use their own domain names. At no time did the government seek any competitive bids to determine the prices that consumers and business should pay for domain name registrations. As public resentment over the high prices and poor service has grown, the federal government is now trying to find ways to introduce competition.

As the Administration seeks to replace the current NSI monopoly with something new, it is using its earlier mistakes as a rationale for a new government giveaway that could create an entirely new set of governance problems for the public. Currently the Administration is negotiating a transfer of the "A DNS root server" to

ICANN, a private non-profit organization. The new non-profit organization seeks the authority to impose fees on all internet domain names, to set international policy on trademarks and other issues, and to launch an undefined set of policy initiatives that it will fund from fees assessed on domain registrations. This new initiative raises a number of questions regarding its lack of accountability, and it is justified largely on the basis that the NSI monopoly needs to be "fixed." But it is hard to see how the creation of a new unaccountable body constitutes a "fix."

GOVERNMENT RESEARCH AND DEVELOPMENT

The federal government invests tens of billions of dollars annually in research and development (R&D), most prominently through the Department of Defense, the Department of Energy, and the Department of Health and Human Services. These investments lead to new inventions and the awarding of thousands of patents—publicly financed, and frequently publicly owned intellectual property.

Since the early 1980s, the government has routinely given away the fruits of the research it sponsors, granting private corporations exclusive, royalty-free rights to commercialize government-financed inventions while failing to include and/or enforce reasonable pricing requirements in the licenses. The result: a corporate welfare bonanza for biotech, computer, aerospace, pharmaceutical, and other firms.

In the critical area of pharmaceuticals, for example, this research giveaway policy leads to superprofiteering by giant drug manufacturers, who charge unconscionably

high prices for important medicines—costing consumers, and often resulting in the denial of treatments
to consumers who are unable to pay high prices. In an
irony that must keep the staff of the Pharmaceutical
Researchers and Manufacturers Association in stitches,
perhaps the largest ripped-off consumer is the federal
government—the same federal government that paid for
the drugs' invention—which must pay extravagant fees
through the Veterans' Administration and Medicaid
(although the government-brokered prices are lower than
those paid by individuals).

It wasn't always so. Following the creation of a major
federal role in research sponsorship in World War II, the
Justice Department concluded in 1947 that "where
patentable inventions are made in the course of per-
forming a Government-financed contract for research
and development, the public interest requires that all
rights to such inventions be assigned to the Government
and not left to the private ownership of the contractor."
The Justice Department recommended also that "as a
basic policy all Government-owned inventions should
be made fully, freely and unconditionally available to the
public without charge, by public dedication or by royalty-free, non-exclusive licensing."[32]

The Justice Department offered what remains a compelling case for non-exclusive licensing: "Public control
will assure free and equal availability of the inventions
to American industry and science; will eliminate any
competitive advantage to the contractor chosen to perform the research work; will avoid undue concentration
of economic power in the hands of a few large corporations; will tend to increase and diversify available
research facilities within the United States to the advan-

tage of the Government and of the national economy; and will thus strengthen our American system of free, competitive enterprise."

Even in 1947, the Justice Department position was not the uniform standpoint of the federal government. The Defense Department consistently maintained a policy of allowing contractors to gain title to government-sponsored inventions, so long as the Pentagon was able to maintain a royalty-free right to use the invention.

In the ensuing decades, government policy evolved unevenly between different agencies, with some gradual increase in exclusive rights transfers to private parties. The various agency policies favoring exclusive licensing were done without Congressional authorization. Seven Members of Congress and Public Citizen filed suit in 1974 against the disposition of government property without Congressional authorization, but the case was dismissed procedurally on lack of standing grounds.

Beginning in the mid-1970s, however, big business, in collaboration with partners at major research universities, began lobbying for a major transformation in government patent policy. Based on highly questionable evidence, the business-university alliance argued that exclusive licensing was necessary to spur private sector innovation and development of government-funded inventions.

The concerted business-university campaign succeeded in 1980 with passage of the Bayh-Dole Act, which transferred exclusive control over many government-sponsored inventions to universities and small business contractors. Universities were in turn permitted to exclusively license to private corporations, including big businesses.

The Bayh-Dole Act was contentious at the time of passage. Other alternatives proposed at the time included a suggestion by Admiral Hyman Rickover that government inventions be licensed non-exclusively for a period of six months; and that if no party had indicated an interest in commercialization, that the patent then be open to competitive bidding for an exclusive license. A proposal by President Carter, which passed the House of Representatives prior to passage of the Bayh-Dole Act, would have limited the exclusive license granted by government to designated "fields of use." But presented with the Bayh-Dole Act, President Carter signed it.

In 1983, President Reagan issued a Presidential memorandum that instructed executive agencies to grant exclusive rights to inventions to contractors of all sizes.

In 1986, Congress passed the Federal Technology Transfer Act, which authorized federal laboratories to enter into exclusive contracts with corporations to develop and market inventions originating in the federal labs. The federal labs have enormous discretion in working out exclusive licensing arrangements and, without even the universities' interest in earning some reasonable royalty, the labs have effectively given away hugely profitable taxpayer-financed inventions with no public return either in the form of royalties or, more importantly, meaningful restraints on company pricing.

THE TAXOL CASE

Consider the case of taxol, a leading anti-cancer drug.[33] In January 1991, the National Cancer Institute licensed taxol to Bristol-Myers Squibb. In the Cooperative Research and Development Agreement (CRADA), NCI agreed to abandon its model "reasonable pricing" language. Instead, it used the following:

> NCI has a concern that there be a reasonable relationship between the pricing of Taxol, the public investment in Taxol research and development, and the health and safety needs of the public. Bristol-Myers Squibb acknowledges that concern, and agrees that these factors will be taken into account in establishing a fair market price for Taxol.

This exhortatory phrasing set the stage for Bristol-Myers Squibb's profiteering.

Bristol-Myers Squibb now markets Taxol at a wholesale price that is nearly 20 times its manufacturing cost. A single injection of Taxol can cost patients considerably more than $2,000—and treatment requires multiple injections.

That NCI gave such total control of pricing decisions to Bristol-Myers Squibb is all the more remarkable because of the extraordinarily minor contribution that the company made to the development of the drug (BMS would claim it has done important collateral research). NCI discovered, manufactured, and tested Taxol in humans. BMS's only contribution to the New Drug Application (NDA) to the Food and Drug Administration was to provide 17 kilograms of Taxol to NCI and to process paperwork. The value of the 17 kilograms was probably less than $5 million. Bristol-Myers did not pay any fee to NCI in entering into the CRADA, and it does not pay royalties to the U.S. government on its billion dollar annual sales revenue from Taxol.

Bristol-Myers Squibb maintains exclusive rights over Taxol due to its control over the health registration data (clinical trial data used for regulatory approval of pharmaceutical drugs), which it gained as a result of the CRADA. The company does not have a patent on the drug, because it was invented by federal researchers. Bristol-Myers Squibb is now leading a major effort—in the United States and around the world—to extend the period during which it maintains exclusive control over the data submitted to receive FDA approval. A National Economic Research Associates study found the consumer cost of an additional two years of Bristol-Myers market exclusivity for Taxol will be $1.27 billion, including $288 million paid by Medicare. Some of those without insurance are simply unable to afford the drug. The cost of preventing generic competition throughout much of the rest of the world is to deny most patients access to the medicine altogether.

Though particularly stark, the Taxol case is not unique. Because the federal government is responsible for the resources leading to the invention of a very high percentage of the most important new drugs, especially anti-cancer drugs, the problem of government licensing is frequently posed.[34]

Where the government hands an annual billion-dollar revenue earner to a private company for a pittance, is it too much to ask the relevant federal agency to enforce reasonable pricing requirements?

This corporate welfare boondoggle has cost consumers hundreds of millions of dollars and almost certainly resulted in treatment denied and a failure to avert preventable cancer deaths. Shame clearly will not work as a disciplinary force to limit corporate welfare abuses.

THE PARTNERSHIP FOR A NEW GENERATION OF VEHICLES (PNGV)

The Partnership for a New Generation of Vehicles (PNGV) is a public/private partnership between seven federal agencies and 20 federal laboratories, and the big three automakers—General Motors, Ford, and what is now DaimlerChrysler. According to the Department of Commerce, the PNGV "aims to strengthen America's competitiveness by developing technologies for a new generation of vehicles." The program was announced on September 29, 1993 by President Clinton, Vice President Gore and the CEOs of the domestic auto makers.

PNGV's main long term goal is to develop a "Supercar," which is described as "an environmentally friendly car with up to triple the fuel efficiency of today's midsize cars—that doesn't sacrifice affordability, performance, or safety." The program represents an effort to coordinate the transfer of property rights for federally funded research and development to the automotive industry. The agencies involved include the Department of Commerce, the Department of Defense (U.S. Army Tank Automotive Research, Development, and Engineering Center and the Advanced Research Projects Agency), the Department of Energy (various national laboratories), the Department of Transportation (including the National Highway and Traffic Safety Administration, the Research and Special Projects Administration, and the Federal Transit Administration), the Environmental Protection Agency (the National Vehicle and Fuel Emissions Laboratory), NASA,and the National Science Foundation.

It is hard to imagine an industry less in need of government support for research than the highly capitalized auto industry, which is reporting record profits year after year. Ford pulled in profits of $5.4 billion in the first three quarters of 1999. GM earned $4.8 billion over the same period. The government is supporting research that the industry would or should do on its own in response to market demands, or could easily be required to do in order to meet tougher environmental standards.

The program also poses the issue of the terms under which patents and other taxpayer-funded intellectual property are transferred to Ford, Chrysler, General Motors, and other large firms. This poses the same problems of monopolistic or oligopolistic control over government-funded research as the biomedical research example, and, if any part of the program is deemed worthy of preservation, similar calls for remedies of nonexclusive licenses. The PNGV program is clouded by secrecy, with negotiations over these and other important issues undertaken in secret, with no public comment.[35]

The structure of the PNGV program creates special anti-competitive problems. The program gives participants an effective exemption from antitrust laws, even though competition in research and development is more likely to yield innovation than bureaucratized collaborative arrangements such as the PNGV initiative.

History provides a clear warning against such arrangements. In the 1960s, the Justice Department filed suit against the automakers for product fixing—for refusing to introduce air quality enhancing technologies. It is instructive to review excerpts from the complaint in the case. It alleged that the U.S. automakers and their trade association had conspired "(a) to eliminate all competition among themselves in the research, development, manufacture and installation of motor vehicle air pollution control equipment; and (b) to eliminate competition in the purchase of patents and patent rights from other parties covering motor vehicle air pollution control equipment."[36] The auto companies subsequently signed a consent decree that stipulated they would not engage in collusive behavior among themselves and their trade association. The Reagan Administration released the car makers from the consent decree; and now the Clinton Administration, acting as if the collusive history never occurred and was not known, has waived antitrust laws and assisted the automakers in resuming non-competitive research and development.

Today, the PNGV initiative is serving as a smokescreen behind which the automakers hide to protect themselves from more stringent air quality standards. U.S. fuel efficiency standards (known as CAFE) have stagnated under the Clinton Administration, even as global warming and rising gas prices demand sharp improvements in auto fuel efficiency. "Cynics think that the PNGV was simply a politically astute 10-year reprieve for the domestic auto industry from threats of higher Corporate Average Fuel Efficiency standards," writes Earth Day founder Denis Hayes in his book, *The Official Earth Day Guide to Planet Repair*. (Exacerbating the problem, the Green Scissors Coalition points out, is the fact that the Department of Energy's expenditures on diesel vehicles directs funding into a highly polluting technology.) Deployment of existing technologies could dramatically enhance auto fuel efficiency and reduce greenhouse gas emissions, but the automakers choose not to make these technologies widely available. Notably, the PNGV program itself does not require the deployment in mass production of the technologies it seeks to develop. The leading innovators in fuel efficiency have been Toyota and Honda, which notably do not participate in the PNGV program. Progress from the PNGV participants only seems to come in response to new announcements from non-participants—again illustrating the importance of competition.[37]

Despite the failures and setbacks of the PNGV, the Clinton Administration is set to replicate it in a truck research program—a way to avoid coming to terms with the poor fuel efficiency of the SUVs and light trucks that now make up about half of U.S. vehicle sales.

SOLUTIONS

The PNGV is not the only example of a federal research program that should be eliminated. Research and development programs in areas like fossil fuel (among them the clean coal technology program, and the Department of Energy's coal and petroleum R&D programs) and nuclear power (the Nuclear Energy Research Initiative) invest funds in support of highly capitalized industries to promote undesirable non-renewable technologies. Such programs are not defensible.

More interesting questions arise in areas where the government is legitimately involved in the research and development sphere, such as in biomedical research. There are several potential ways to resolve the giveaway problem embedded in current policy.

One way is to revitalize the Rickover proposal of immediate non-exclusive licensing, followed by the possibility of exclusive licensing if no party accepts a non-exclusive license. This arrangement would guarantee competition and keep prices down. If exclusive licensing proves necessary, in a Rickover-style scheme or otherwise, the license should be granted on the basis of an auction. The auction should consider factors such as: the strongest guarantees of low price marketing of the final product, buyer commitment to invest profits in research and development, and royalties to the government. The weight attached to these factors should perhaps vary according to the type of invention. For example, in the case of pharmaceuticals, reasonable pricing should take priority over royalty returns to the government.

Federal agencies should be able to adopt these policies on their own, but the recent history of cozy relationships between manufacturers, universities and federal laboratories has led federal agencies and universities alike to cut sweetheart deals that boost corporate profits while punishing consumers and failing to recoup government investments. Congressional action is needed, and citizens should be guaranteed procedural opportunities to challenge sweetheart arrangements that do not comport with statutory requirements.

BAILOUTS

The modern corporate bailout period began with the 1974 Lockheed bailout, escalated with the 1979 Chrysler bailout, and soared with the gigantic savings-and-loan bailouts of the late 1980s and early 1990s.

These bailouts, of course, are generally doled out to large corporations and industries. When a family-owned restaurant fails, no government intervenes to stop it from going belly up. If a small factory can't pay its bills, it goes out of business. The bailout, a premier form of corporate welfare, is typically yet another market distortion against the interests of small and medium-sized businesses.

BAILOUT LESSONS

Bailouts are different from other corporate welfare categories in that they are ad hoc and unplanned. There is no ongoing government bailout program to be cancelled or reformed.

But there are lessons to draw from recent bailout experience that should inform Congressional action now and in the future.

First is the issue of payback. In the case of the Chrysler bailout, the federal government received warrants and ultimately earned a profit on its loans. In the case of the S&Ls, a special levy was assessed against the industry to pay some of the costs—although the overwhelming majority of the cost was borne by the taxpayers. If Congress determines in any particular case that a company or industry bailout is necessary, it should prioritize the issue of payback—assuring that, after the company or industry is nursed back to health, our government is paid in full, or as close to full as possible.

Second, monetary payback is not enough. In bailouts, the government is stepping in because private financial markets are not willing to invest in or make loans to the troubled corporate entity or entities. And especially because the government is doing more than making a market-justified loan, it has a right to make additional non-monetary demands, particularly demands designed to prevent the need for future bailouts.

In the case of the S&L bailout, consumer groups repeatedly urged Congress to require depository institutions, as a condition of the bailout, to carry notices in their monthly balance statements. These notices would have invited consumers to join democratically run, non-profit, non-partisan consumer groups that would advocate for their interests and provide an institutionalized scrutiny of S&Ls, banks, and other depository institutions.[38] These organizations would have been privately funded, voluntary, and statewide. They would have operated at no cost to the taxpayer or to corporations, because their mailing inserts (paid for by the consumer group) would have used the "extra" portion of the billing envelope, adding no postage costs to the S&Ls. These finan-

cial consumer groups would have functioned as an institutionalized early warning system, ringing alarm bells
over emerging problems before they reached crisis phase.
They remain a vital proposal for depository institutions,
as does the proposal more generally for other industries
and companies. At minimum, some variant of this proposal should be attached to every bailout, and where
applicable, as in the case of the digital TV spectrum, to
giveaways also.

Third, the S&L crisis was triggered in large part by
industry deregulation, specifically the Reagan Administration's decision to permit S&Ls to raise interest rates
and to leave their area of competence (lending for housing) and venture into other uncharted, riskier waters.[39]
And it was caused, to some considerable extent, by S&L
criminal activity. This experience should be an important
cautionary note for corporate welfare opponents, including conservatives who fancy themselves opposed to "Big
Government": deregulation, underregulation and non-
regulation pave the way for bailouts, especially in the
financial sector. The non-regulated world of hedge funds,
for example, contains all the warning signs of eventual
crisis and a demand for bailouts. The perceived need for
Federal Reserve intervention in the case of Long-Term
Capital Management, and the possibility that losses to
the firm could have been much more severe, highlights
the potentially serious bailout possibilities that might be
faced in the near future, absent newly imposed regulations.

Finally, strong antitrust policy and enforcement is a
vital prophylactic against the emergence of too-big-to-
fail institutions which, by their very size and importance
to the national economy, are sure to benefit from a government bailout in he face of potential collapse.

The passage in 1999 of HR 10, which erased the line, established by the Glass-Steagall Act and the Bank Holding Company Act, preventing common ownership of banks, insurance companies and securities firms will exacerbate the too-big-to-fail syndrome. The removal of barriers to common ownership in the United States is triggering a global financial consolidation leading to the creation of giant financial conglomerates. Citigroup—the product of the merger between Citibank and Travelers Insurance—is the preeminent example. (The Citigroup merger occurred before the passage of HR 10, but became legal only with its enactment; the merged conglomerate had been operating on a temporary waiver of rules proscribing such a corporate marriage.)

With the new financial mergers, the bailout concerns extend beyond just the too-big-to-fail phenomenon. Regulators are likely to fear that permitting, say, an insurance company to fail would endanger the health of its conglomerate parent, which would in turn threaten a crisis of the entire financial sector, including taxpayer-insured banks. That will create strong pressure for a federal bailout. HR 10 will also effectively function to extend the federal safety net to non-bank affiliates of federally insured banks. If a bank with a failing insurance affiliate makes bad loans in order bail out the insurance company, and then itself faces financial trouble as a result, federal deposit insurance will be there to back up the bank.

That insurance comes cheap. In 1995, the Federal Deposit Insurance Corporation (FDIC) stopped collecting deposit insurance premiums from banks. Today, all banks, except for a handful of the most risk-prone, receive free insurance from the federal government. As a result, the bank insurance fund at FDIC has only about $32 billion on hand to cover all contingencies for nearly 9,000 commercial banks with almost $3 trillion in deposits. And should FDIC come up short when banks fail in an economic downturn, it can turn to the U.S. treasury. In 1991, with the bank insurance fund in the red, Congress voted to establish a $30 billion contingency fund at the Treasury Department to be used in the event that FDIC ran out of deposit insurance money.

SPECIAL BAILOUT PROBLEMS

The S&L looters are back. A federal judge in California has ruled that Congress broke the government's contract with Glendale Federal Bank when capital based on goodwill was outlawed in the 1989 savings and loan reform legislation.[40] The court awarded the corporation $908.9 million. There are some 125 suits pending with claims similar to those of Glendale. If the Glendale case is a precedent, the government could lose another $30 billion on top of the nearly $500 billion in principal and interest that has already been obligated in the S&L bailout, with some of the new corporate welfare benefits conferred, as the *New York Times* has pointed out, on some of the more notorious figures in the savings and loan debacle, including some who are serving prison terms.[41] The 1989 reform legislation properly insisted that failed institutions be closed and that remaining S&Ls have adequate capital—actual capital, not the fake capital represented by something as vague as goodwill.

The Glendale case presents two problems. One is how vigorously the Clinton Administration Justice Department is contesting the Glendale line of cases. The second issue is how the Glendale claims will be paid, if in fact courts hold that they must be. The *New York Times* reports that a provision was inserted into last fall's omnibus appropriations bill—without hearings or open debate, in yet another example of how corporate welfare giveaways are bound up with anti-democratic procedures—that was designed to allay fears of lobbyists that the Treasury Department might refuse to pay or that the industry might end up being saddled with the costs through a special assessment.[42] This provision must be repealed, and it should be promptly replaced with legislation that assesses the special fee the industry opposes. The 1989 reform effort, including the implementation of strict capital rules and the elimination of worthless imitation capital like goodwill restored confidence in the savings and loan industry. This restoration of confidence has been a sizable government benefit, courtesy of the taxpayers, to the entire financial industry and its shareholders, and particularly to the thrift sector. It would be wrong for the taxpayers, who have borne the brunt of the savings and loan bailout, to now be required to pay the judgments of these goodwill suits.

And now another set of corporate rogues—the tobacco pushers—may be set to avail themselves of a bailout stratagem. The normal course for a company that cannot pay its bills is not to turn to the government, but to enter into Chapter 11, temporary bankruptcy. Since the 1979 reforms to the bankruptcy laws, large corporations have increasingly used bankruptcy as a refuge from large civil liability claims. A.H. Robins, Johns Manville, Union Carbide, and Dow Corning are among the companies which have followed this route,[43] and Big Tobacco is now waving the threat of bankruptcy to strengthen its bargaining position in lawsuits and in the legislative process. These companies have manipulated the bankruptcy code to force victims of dangerous products or dangerous production processes to absorb some substantial portion of the costs of their injuries and to separate future income streams from liability. This manipulation is particularly outrageous because it involves not financial creditors who misassessed the viability of a bankrupt company's operation, but innocent victims of corporate violence. There is, in the process, no government transfer to private corporations, but it is the law which permits these companies to victimize consumers twice, first by injuring them and secondly by denying them adequate compensation through the bankruptcy ploy. A recent U.S. Supreme Court decision[44] should work to diminish corporations' ability to abuse bankruptcy procedures, but legislative reforms are needed as well. And careful monitoring is needed of the tobacco industry's ploys, especially as Big Tobacco faces billion-dollar verdicts in Florida and elsewhere for years of lying and manipulating nicotine levels to addict millions to the deadly smoking habit. A declaration of bankruptcy by the tobacco companies may not be bad for public health, but history certainly shows it would pose serious risks.

CORPORATE TAX EXPENDITURES

Federal corporate tax expenditures—special exclusions, exemptions, deductions, credits, deferrals, or tax rates —totaled more than $76 billion in fiscal year 1999, according to conservative estimates by the Office of Management and Budget. For the five-year period 2000-2004, the government will spend more than $394 billion on corporate tax subsidies.[45]

The notion of tax "expenditure" expresses the idea that revenue losses due to preferential tax provisions such as special exclusions, exemptions, deductions, credits, deferrals, or tax rates have the same budgetary implication as a giveaway of government resources. When the government does not collect certain taxes due to tax expenditures, it is spending money. And when the government fails to collect taxes from corporations due to various legal preferences, it is subsidizing those companies as surely as if it were making direct payments to them. The issue here is not tax rates, but tax preferences for particular categories of corporations or corporate behavior.

The special insidiousness of corporate tax expenditures is that they are hidden subsidies. They do not appear as budget expenditures, and because they represent money not collected (rather than payments doled out) they do not generate even the felt-outrage of off-budget giveaways. Generally, once they have been included in the Internal Revenue Code, corporate tax expenditures remain on the books unless Congress affirmatively acts to remove them. This situation contrasts to on-budget programs, which require continuing Congressional approval and authorizations to continue, and therefore are automatically subject to ongoing Congressional review, if not action.

The 1974 Budget Act requires that a list of tax expenditures, corporate and individual, be included in the budget. This budgetary requirement at least makes it possible to identify the cost of most corporate tax expenditures, and it is a model for what should be done in other corporate welfare areas.

Many of the corporate tax breaks merit special attention because they actually encourage undesirable activity, including environmentally destructive activity. The oil and gas industry, for example, wins major subsidies through the tax code. When the need to encourage a transition to renewable fuels is clear, why does the Internal Revenue Code encourage more aggressive oil drilling, with its associated environmental harms, than even market demand would induce? What rationale is there for artificially biasing the market against conservation and efficiency? Tax escapes and credits to the oil and gas industry take more than $500 million from taxpayers annually.[46]

Similarly, several tax rules encourage wanton mining, beyond that which is justified even on market terms, by providing tax incentives for mining operations. The effect is to bias the market against recycling interests.[47] The percentage depletion allowance for mining allows mining companies to deduct a certain percentage from their gross income that exceeds the actual loss of value. (These vary by mineral, with sulfur, uranium, and lead given the high percentage of 22 percent.) Rules that allow immediate expensing of exploration and development, rather than a write-off as mines are depleted, plus other mining tax escapes, cost the Treasury an estimated $300 million a year.[48]

Then there are the specially targeted loopholes, such as the Amway example mentioned in the introduction. The Amway case is typical in the shady fashion in which it transpired, but it is somewhat atypical in that the exact beneficiaries were identifiable. Anonymity works as a protective shield for the corporate tax renegades. Removing that anonymity would make preservation of the tax advantages much more difficult politically. The President's Office of Management and Budget (OMB) should be required to compile a list of the top 50 beneficiaries of each corporate tax expenditure.

A second critical issue involves the intended effect of each tax expenditure. Aside from serving as payoffs to politically well-connected companies, tax expenditures are designed to encourage specific kinds of behavior. Do they do so?[49] For example, the Work Opportunity Tax Credit is designed to encourage firms to hire certain groups of people (such as recent welfare or food stamp recipients) for low-skilled jobs. The FY 1999 cost of this corporate tax expenditure is $285 million.[50] But it may be that the tax credit also provides an incentive for churning of these employees, so that employers can repeatedly recoup the tax incentive. (Employers can claim a credit of up to $2,400 for the first $6,000 of a workers earnings; workers must be employed for at least 400 hours for the credit to be claimed.) The tax credit may also provide an incentive for employers to replace existing employees with new employees from the targeted groups. Determining whether or not these unintended and undesirable outcomes occur requires more data gathering and close scrutiny. And because of the nature of tax expenditures—they are effectively "administered" by the IRS rather than agencies with expertise in the relevant field—scrutiny will come from Congress, the media and citizens, or not at all.

One way to facilitate that scrutiny is to have sunset provisions for corporate tax expenditures (as for other corporate welfare programs), which would require Congressional renewal of tax breaks. The Work Opportunity Tax Credit is indeed scheduled to be phased out by 2004, but an unproven tax expenditure of this sort should have a shorter first life, say two years. At the least, a short initial period for tax expenditures would allow testing and review of whether they achieved their desired effects, and whether they had any harmful consequences. Generally, and without regard to the Work Opportunity Tax Credit, such a standard seems particularly appropriate given the harsh time limitations applied to welfare for poor people in the 1996 "welfare reforms."

Another area deserving of immediate and priority Congressional investigation is the apparent underpayment of federal income tax by foreign corporations. A recent General Accounting Office (GAO, a Congressional research agency) report concluded that foreign-controlled corporations doing business in the United States pay approximately half the taxes that U.S. companies pay.[51] The report found that the approximately 15,000 large U.S. companies paid an average of $8.1 million in federal income taxes in 1995. The approximately 2,700 large foreign-controlled corporations in the United States paid an average of $4.2 million in the same year. Foreign-controlled companies paid taxes as a percentage of sales at just over half the rate of U.S. companies. Senator Byron Dorgan and Citizens for Tax Justice attribute the differential payments in large part to manipulative transfer pricing by foreign multinationals—this practice of dubious legality involves paying too little or charging too much in paper transactions between U.S. and foreign affiliates, so that the income of the U.S. affiliate is artificially lowered. Citizens for Tax Justice points out that the growing number of foreign corporate takeovers of U.S. companies (Daimler's purchase of Chrysler, Deutche Bank's takeover of Bankers Trust and BP's buyout of Amoco and possibly Arco prominent among them) may accentuate the tax avoidance problem.[52]

A second, growing source of multinational tax avoidance, according to Citizens for Tax Justice, involves financial transactions. In one, newly invented shell game, companies pay interest to non-taxable offshore subsidiaries and deduct the interest payments against their worldwide taxable income. But they claim an exemption from U.S. anti-tax haven laws by contending that, for U.S. tax purposes, the interest earned by the offshore subsidiaries does not exist. The Treasury Department has tried to clamp down on this tax-avoidance scheme, but has been blocked by Congress.

INSURANCE SCHEMES, FORMAL AND DE FACTO

One of the overriding trends in corporate welfare in recent decades has been the socialization of risk. In making risky investments—some socially desirable, some not—and sometimes undertaking reckless activities, investors are attracted to the prospect of high returns on investment. But corporations are increasingly brazen about foisting the risk of failure—the very reason for high returns—on taxpayers and consumers.

The drive to socialize risk while privatizing profit is evident in the corporate drive for tort reform, the tobacco companies' effort in recent years to limit their civil liability, and in the vital importance that business attaches to government insurance schemes, formal and de facto. Among these are: the International Monetary Fund, the Exchange Stabilization Fund (ESF) and the insurance scheme of the Price Anderson Act.

Given the existence of a thriving private insurance market, there should be some skepticism attached to claims of necessity of any public insurance scheme. Certainly, there are cases where public insurance programs, voluntary or involuntary, may be merited. Where there is a public interest in guaranteeing industry survival and stability, for example, public insurance schemes may be sound public policy, especially where there is a likelihood of government bailout in the event of major industry liability or failure. But even in these cases, there should be a strong presumption of full-cost recovery and the imposition of reciprocal obligations from the insured, upon whom significant benefits (e.g., public confidence) are conferred by public insurance.

Where there is a viable alternative private market, and no clear public interest in industry protection, hard questions should be asked about the appropriateness of public insurance: What is the need for a public insurance alternative in such situations? Does the government do more than provide a subsidized service? Does the government serve as an insurer of last resort—and if so, is this a beneficial public policy or one that merely provides an additional welfare support to other insurers? What public interest is served by government involvement in this area of insurance provision? Does it encourage imprudent investments and actions? Why should the government charge less than market rates for the insurance it provides? Is it a lead in to later government bailouts, as has been the case with banks?

THE IMF AND THE ESF

The IMF is an international financial agency located in Washington, D.C., that helps debtor countries overcome balance of payments deficits. It makes loans to countries, conditioned on those countries adopting a policy package known as "structural adjustment." In recent years, the IMF has expanded its traditional function to function as a de facto insurer of the global financial system, making massive loans to countries that suffer from sudden withdrawals of international capital.

The Exchange Stabilization Fund is an off-budget account controlled by the Secretary of Treasury. Congress established it to enable the Secretary to defend the dollar in the event it lost an excessive amount of its value relative to other leading currencies. In recent years, the Secretary has made very large draws on the ESF to fund U.S. participation in bailouts of countries that are suffering from financial meltdowns.

The vast shifts in international financial capital which have characterized the global financial markets in the last decade have resulted in episodic crises when currency traders, operating in herd-like fashion, suddenly act to pull money out of an economy. These are typically national economies in which there has been a recent, prior infusion of foreign capital in a speculative frenzy. In the last five years, the most severe of these crises have occurred in Mexico, South Korea, Thailand, Indonesia, and Russia.

In simple terms, the selloff of a country's currency forces its devaluation, making it relatively more expensive to pay debts owed in foreign currencies, and leaving the country with massive debt payment obligations that it is unable to meet.

When individuals are unable to pay their debts, of course, typically the debtor and the creditor share the pain. Through bankruptcy or otherwise, a process of work-out occurs, with the creditors receiving less than full repayment. This equitably distributes responsibility for overborrowing to the debtor and to the creditor for imprudent lending.

No such thing happens in international financial markets. When countries are suddenly unable to meet their payment obligations, the IMF rushes in. It provides money to the borrower, often in packages which include large contributions from the ESF. This money is used to repay creditors, letting them off the hook. The pain is borne exclusively by the borrowing country, which must accept recessionary austerity conditions (including tax increases, harsh budget cuts and government layoffs) from the IMF as a condition for the bailout of its private creditors.

Of course, the story varies from bailout to bailout, but this is the essential process.

In 1995, the Clinton Administration orchestrated a nearly $50 billion bailout of the Wall Street interests which stood to lose billions with the Mexican peso devaluation. The centerpiece of the bailout was $20 billion in currency swaps, loans and loan guarantees from the ESF. The IMF (in which the U.S. maintains an 18 percent share) contributed almost $18 billion to the bailout. Not all of the $50 billion was used, and what was used was paid back, but that does not affect the character of the Administration's action as providing after-the-fact insurance.

The peso devaluation was necessitated by Mexico's chronic balance of payments deficit, but the severity of the devaluation and subsequent crisis stemmed from the Mexican government's long maintenance of an overvalued peso. Fully aware of the peso's overvaluation,[53] foreign lenders and short-term investors continued to flock to the Mexican market because of its high, 18 percent interest rates. When the inevitable devaluation occurred, investors pulled out en masse. Rather than letting Wall Street accept responsibility for irresponsible lending, the Clinton Administration, with the help of the IMF, orchestrated the bailout.

The Mexico crisis repeated itself in Asia in 1997. Foreign investors and lenders poured money into the Asian tigers to take advantage of very high interest rates and returns, and then withdrew in herdlike fashion when the bubble burst. With South Korea, Thailand, the Philippines, Malaysia, and Indonesia unable to pay back foreign loans (which suddenly appeared more expensive following devaluation), the IMF took the lead role in organizing bailouts of creditors and investors.

IMF loans injected money into the Asian economies to enable them to pay back their foreign debts. The amounts at stake were not insignificant: U.S. banks' exposure in South Korea was estimated to total more than $10 billion. BankAmerica alone reportedly had more than $3 billion in outstanding loans to South Korean firms, and Citicorp more than $2 billion. The other major U.S. banks with outstanding loans to South Korea included J.P. Morgan, Bankers Trust, the Bank of New York and Chase Manhattan.[54] Instead of eating their losses, the banks which made bad loans in South Korea and elsewhere in Asia received the money owed them, in some cases over modestly extended repayment periods.

The IMF/ESF money goes in and goes out. The banks get their money, the countries contract new debts to the IMF and get stuck with the IMF austerity demands. These recessionary structural adjustment demands have had tragic consequences throughout Asia. In South

Korea, the unemployment rate has skyrocketed from under 3 percent to approaching 10 percent. In Indonesia, economic contraction has eradicated the income growth of the last three decades, with poverty rates soaring from 11 to 40 percent.[55]

There is still more. Among the conditions imposed on the Asian countries by the IMF and Rubin are requirements that these countries open up their economies further to foreign investors. (These demands relate to foreign "direct investment" in factories, agriculture, and service operations ranging from tourism to banks, not just "portfolio" investment in stocks, bonds, and currency.) Treasury Secretary Robert Rubin specifically and successfully pressured South Korea to open up its financial sector.

As a result, the very U.S. banks that contributed to South Korea's crisis and received a U.S. taxpayer bailout now stand to buy up lucrative sectors of the South Korean economy. Similar demands have successfully been made in other troubled Asian countries.[56]

History repeated itself a few months later, this time as farce, in Russia. Despite a widespread understanding that Russia had fallen into the grips of an unmitigated criminal capitalism, foreign capital poured into the country, at some points seeking to take advantage of interest rates that hit 100 percent. No one could have doubted the risk of lending to Russia. But when the inevitable collapse came, the IMF—prodded by the Clinton Administration—was there with a bailout package. In July, the IMF signed off on a $22 billion bailout. The IMF released $4 billion dollars into the country immediately. That money went to pay back domestic and foreign creditors, with the rest apparently stolen. It served absolutely no purpose but to subsidize the wealthy in and outside of Russia, all of whom had gambled with their investments in an effort to take advantage of the extraordinary interest offered. In August, Russia defaulted on its loans, and the IMF suspended the bailout.

Not only is the double subsidy to the Big Banks unjust, it helps perpetuate the very problem it is designed to remedy. When the IMF and the Treasury Department bail out the banks—in effect providing free insurance—it sends a message: "Don't worry about the downside of your international loans. As long as enough banks get in too deep, we'll rescue you at the end of the day." That encourages more reckless bank lending, since the banks can earn high interest on high risk loans without having to absorb losses. (Economists call this the "moral hazard" problem.) While consumers don't benefit from the higher bank profits, they frequently find themselves hit with higher charges when banks suffer losses from reckless lending that are not fully bailed out.

Working out a sensible system of international financial regulation, which avoids Wall Street bailouts and the unfairly punishing of debtor countries is a complicated matter. It is clear, however, that the IMF and the ESF have to be reined in. Indeed, even the *Wall Street Journal* and Wall Street conservatives such as George Schultz, William Simon and Walter Wriston have suggested the IMF's powers should be restricted or the Fund abolished altogether.[57]

The Republican majority on the International Financial Institution Advisory Commission (the Meltzer Commission, a Congressionally appointed panel) recommended a series of intriguing proposals to restrict IMF lending to avoid the moral hazard problem.[58] At minimum the IMF should be denied all new funds.

Second, Congressional authorization should be required for ESF expenditures of larger than $100 million. Representative Bernard Sanders has introduced legislation to require a Congressional vote prior to ESF expenditures over a specified amount.

NUCLEAR INSURANCE: THE PRICE-ANDERSON ACT

The nuclear industry may be the most subsidized in U.S. history. It is completely a product of U.S. government research and development. Having emerged from massive government investments, the nuclear industry has never cut its umbilical cord tie to the government.[59]

One critical, ongoing support for the industry is the Price-Anderson Indemnity Act, which limits the liability of the nuclear industry (both plant operators, and suppliers and vendors) in the event of a major nuclear accident. Under Price-Anderson, each utility is required to maintain $200 million in liability insurance per reactor. If claims following an accident exceed that amount, all other nuclear operators are required to pay up to $83.9 million for each reactor they operate. Under the terms of Price-Anderson, neither the owner of a unit which has a major accident nor the entire utility can be held liable for more than these sums. As of August 1998, this system capped insurance coverage for any accident at $9.43 billion.[60]

When the Price-Anderson Act was adopted in 1957, at the dawn of the commercial nuclear industry, "the Act was intended to overcome reluctance to participate [in the transition to private nuclear industry] by the

nascent industry worried by the possibility of cata-
strophic, uninsured claims resulting from a large nuclear
accident."[61] Leaving aside for the moment the ecologi-
cal and economic risks which should disqualify continuation of, let alone support for, the nuclear industry,
assume that such a rationale was defensible at the time,
as the government tried to promote development of an
energy source which many believed would be safe, cheap,
and abundant.

But watch how the rationalization perpetuates itself.
"By 1965," the NRC reports, "when the first 10-year
extension of the Act was being considered, a handful of
nuclear power reactors was coming into operation, and
the nuclear industry considered itself on the verge of
expanding into large-scale nuclear power generation.
Thus, the need for continued operation of the Price-
Anderson system for the forthcoming 10 years was
believed to be critical for the unrestricted development
of nuclear power."[62]

A decade later, when another extension of the Act was
being considered, the industry was more buoyantly opti-
mistic than it ever had been or would be again. "With
dozens of plants in operation or under construction and
with hundreds more being contemplated to be in operation by the end of the century," the industry urged that
the Act be extended rapidly so that "any uncertainty
about extension would not disrupt nuclear power development,"[63] says the NRC.

Now the industry is in decline. There have been no
new orders for nuclear plants for the past 25 years, and
aging plants are beginning to be shuttered. The original
rationale for the Act is no longer plausible. But nothing
has changed with respect to Price Anderson. Indeed, the

NRC argues, "Given industry perception of the continuing need for Price-Anderson, and in view of the lack of new orders in plants, the situation is in some respects similar to what it was when Congress saw the need for enactment of the original Price-Anderson Act."[64]

(In one way, things are worse than they were in 1957: with nuclear plants closing due to aging, safety concerns, inefficiency, and license expiration, the Price-Anderson liability cap will progressively decline in future years. If the upper end of nuclear plant closing projections occurs, available insurance funds could shrink to $4.5 billion in 2013.[65])

The industry has gone through a full life cycle, but somehow it never outgrew the need for a federal insurance scheme and liability cap. The result has been a massive subsidy to nuclear power companies. Using the NRC's conservative numbers for the upper limit on a worst-case scenario accident and on the probability of such an accident occurring, Professors Jeffrey Dubin and Geoffrey Rothwell estimated the cumulative Price-Anderson subsidy to the nuclear industry through 1988 to be $111 billion in 1985 dollars.[66] This estimate is based on NRC data on the cost of worst-case accidents—data which is conservative because it does not include health effects.

If, again, we leave aside the demerits of nuclear power, there could be justification for a federal scheme to promote risk sharing in a context which poses a (hypothetically) very small chance of an extremely large loss. (It should be emphasized, however, that this is exactly the situation for which the private insurance and reinsurance markets are designed.) But there is no justification for combining such a scheme with an overall liability cap.

The $9.4 billion liability is nowhere near sufficient to pay for the human health and property damages that could result from a nuclear meltdown. Nuclear Regulatory Commission studies have estimated costs in a worst-case scenario at more than $300 billion for a single catastrophe.[67]

The nuclear industry's real insurance program is not the $9.4 billion scheme of Price-Anderson, but the free insurance provided by the public. In the event of a catastrophic accident, after the $9.4 billion was spent, it is the federal government that would inevitably cover the costs—with some costs probably absorbed by victims who have their injuries compounded by inadequate compensation.

Price-Anderson is a textbook example of the hybrid insurance-liability cap program that should be prohibited *per se*.

"Many nuclear suppliers express the view that without Price-Anderson coverage, they would not participate in the nuclear industry," reports the NRC.[68] If an industry which has benefited from massive government research and development and other subsidies for more than four decades, and which creates staggering, environmentally dangerous waste disposal problems and poses enormous risks to human health, cannot survive without government support, then it should not survive. The nuclear industry cannot meet the market insurance test and, with substitute energy sources available, it is not needed. The Price Anderson Act expires in 2002. If it is not repealed before then, it should not be renewed. If nuclear facilities close as a result, well, occasionally at least, corporate America should be subjected to the widely touted rigors of a free market.

GOVERNMENT SPONSORED ENTERPRISES

Government sponsored enterprises (GSEs) are stealth recipients of corporate welfare. Instead of cash or federal tax subsidies, GSEs like Fannie Mae and Freddie Mac receive their government largesse in the less obvious form of credit enhancements.

Thanks to their extensive links to the federal government, Fannie and Freddie borrow money in the markets at almost the same rate as the U.S. Treasury, something that no competitor can come close to matching.

Like other GSEs, much of the risk of these housing finance enterprises remains with the federal government while the profits flow to private shareholders.

It is true that the secondary market operations of these GSEs provide an important service by improving access to mortgage credit by home buyers and stabilizing the mortgage market. The GSEs obtain funds from the bond markets and acquire mortgages from local lenders. The process ensures that home buyers can tap into the nation's savings pool for mortgage financing.

Could these functions be carried out without government subsidy? Could private corporations—without links to the government and without corporate welfare—perform the same functions? These are questions meriting close Congressional scrutiny.

The key to Fannie and Freddie's phenomenal profits and soaring stock values is the financial market's perception that there is an implicit government guarantee behind the obligations of these corporations.

There are good reasons for the financial market's belief that the U.S. Treasury and the taxpayers would be the fall guys in the event of a default. Here are some of the GSEs' links to the federal government:

➤ Fannie and Freddie each have a contingency fund of $2.25 billion that can be drawn from the U. S. Treasury.

➤ Their securities are government securities for the purposes of the Securities Exchange Act of 1934.

➤ Their securities serve as eligible collateral for Federal Reserve banks' discount loans.

➤ The securities are exempt from registration under the Securities Act of 1933.

➤ The Secretary of the Treasury approves the issues.

➤ The Federal Reserve is the fiscal agent for the issues.

➤ Their obligations are eligible for unlimited investments by national banks and state bank members of the Federal Reserve as well as by federally insured thrifts.

Both Fannie and Freddie are exempt from local and state taxes—another benefit that clearly falls under the rubric of corporate welfare. (Even when the District of Columbia was struggling on the edge of bankruptcy, Fannie Mae refused to cough up a dollar in lieu of local income taxes.)

There are varying opinions about how much these links, and resulting savings on borrowings, mean to Fannie and Freddie. Fannie Mae Chairman and CEO Franklin Raines concedes there are "benefits" (he prefers the word "benefits" to "subsidies"), but does not assign a dollar figure to the government ties.

However, the Congressional Budget Office (CBO) conducted an extensive study of Fannie and Freddie entitled "Assessing the Public Costs and Benefits of Fannie Mae and Freddie Mac." CBO estimated that the credit enhancement stemming from the government links was at least $6.5 billion in 1995.[69]

According to CBO, Fannie and Freddie pass only part of that subsidy on to home buyers—about $4.4 billion—with the remainder of the credit enhancement subsidy pocketed by private shareholders, the corporations' executives, and lobbyists.[70] In other words, for every two dollars delivered to home buyers, Fannie and Freddie take one dollar of the subsidy for themselves.

CBO estimates that in 1995, about 40 percent of the of the earnings of Fannie and Freddie could be traced to the benefits of their government-sponsored status.[71]

These corporations have prospered under their GSE status and credit enhancement subsidies. Fannie Mae's stock appreciated 1,053 percent between 1989 and 1998. Freddie's stock appreciation was even greater, 1,260 percent. Sixteen years ago, Fannie Mae had a market value of $500 million. Today, the corporation is worth $70 billion.

In the process, Fannie and Freddie have become the dominant force in the housing finance market.

It is obvious that some of the subsidy derived from their GSE status is being used, not for home buyers, but to increase corporate power and control over all facets of the mortgage business.

Will this growing duopoly enjoyed by Fannie and Freddie stifle competition by private companies—competition that might reduce costs and encourage innovation in a variety of mortgage products?

Not only stockholders, but officials of Fannie Mae and Freddie Mac are enriched by the subsidy.

In 1997, for example, Jim Johnson, Fannie Mae's chairman, received $5,441,232 in salary, bonuses, stock options, and other compensation. His predecessor walked away with a whopping severance package worth more than $20 million. Lawrence Small, president and CEO, received salary, bonuses and stock options of $2,948,751 in 1997. Jamie Gorelick, after leaving the Justice Department as deputy attorney general in May 1997, was the recipient of $1,850,993 in salary, bonuses, and stock options as vice chair of Fannie Mae during the last eight months of the year. She had no previous experience in housing finance.

The directors and officers of Fannie and Freddie have long enjoyed lucrative stock options. At the end of 1995, according to the CBO, executive officers and directors of Fannie Mae owned 1.6 million shares of the corporation. In Freddie Mac's case, CBO said executive officers and directors owned 695,000 shares of their corporation. In addition, the compensation agreements with officers of both corporations include generous options on hundreds of thousands of additional shares worth millions of dollars.[72]

All of the government sponsored enterprises are huge issuers of debt. Fannie and Freddie along with two other GSEs—the Federal Home Loan Bank System and the Farm Credit System—issued $1.62 trillion of debt during the first quarter of this year.

The Federal Home Loan Bank System has been under fire from the Treasury Department for its borrowing practices. The FHLB System has used its ability as a GSE to borrow cheaply and engage in arbitrage by making investments in non-housing related investments.

But the champion of the arbitrage games among the GSEs has to be Farmer Mac, the newest addition to the rank of government sponsored enterprises. The General Accounting Office reports that Farmer Mac holds $1.18 billion of investments unrelated to its agricultural finance mission—or 61 percent of its assets.[73]

House Banking Committee Chair Jim Leach calls it "unconscionable" for a government sponsored enterprise to have more than three-fifths of its assets in non-mission related activities.

"When a governmentally-privileged institution, that is established to serve farmers, abuses its status by investing disproportionately in arbitraged financial investments rather than agricultural loans, the Treasury and the Congress have an obligation to review its management practices," Leach says.

Leach is right about Farmer Mac. But Farmer Mac is but one small corner of the GSE story, particularly compared to the mammoth operations like Fannie and Freddie. All of these GSEs enjoy a special status because of their links to the federal government—they all enjoy benefits because of the market's perception that the U.

S. Treasury and the taxpayers stand behind their obligations—a fail-safe status that leaves the federal government with the risk and the shareholders and the GSE
executives with the profits.

A top-to-bottom review is needed of all the government sponsored enterprises. Are these hybrid half government, half private entities needed to meet credit
needs? How well do they meet their statutory missions
in specific sectors? And how much of their operations
are devoted, not to their missions, but to playing the
market in outlandish and unneeded arbitrage games?
How much of their subsidy is used to benefit consumers,
and how much is siphoned into shareholder profits and
bloated executive compensation arrangements? Are
existing capital standards adequate?

Addressing these problems will require confronting
the familiar issue of corporate welfare beneficiaries'
political influence. Some of the GSE subsidies intended
to lower costs for home buyers are being diverted to build
political and lobbying power designed to make it difficult, if not impossible, for the Congress to provide (or
for the public to demand) proper oversight or regulatory
improvements which would protect the public, increase
support for affordable housing, or ensure open competition in the mortgage market.

A report by the Campaign Reform Project reveals that
Fannie and Freddie are some of the largest political soft
money donors—contributing more than $900,000 in the
1997-1998 election cycle. This is in addition to contributions by key employees.

Many of Washington's premier law firms along
with former Members of Congress show up on the GSEs'
list of lobbyists. The lobbying lists have included Ken

Duberstein, former chief of staff to President Reagan, Nicholas Calio, President Bush's Congressional liaison and Michael Boland, former aide to Senate Majority Leader Trent Lott. Former Members of Congress on the GSE lobbying payroll include Senator Steve Symms, Representative Vin Weber and Representative Tom Downey.

EXPORT AND OVERSEAS MARKETING ASSISTANCE

Various government agencies maintain an array of export assistance programs. These programs raise the question of why overseas marketing and lending and other export assistance should be a government rather than private sector function.

As regular beneficiaries of double standards, big business executives and lobbyists, it seems, are without a sense of irony. How do the corporate proponents of international trade agreements designed to promote misnamed "free trade" explain their simultaneous support for marketing subsidies? If it is only on the grounds that "other countries do the same thing," perhaps they should turn their multinational lobbying prowess to eliminating other countries' export assistance programs.

The most disturbing feature of many of the export assistance programs may be that the assisted companies export troublesome products or technologies—weapons, or environmentally hazardous equipment, for example.

Such programs, especially the various private corporate arms exports initiatives supported by the Defense Department, should be ended.

WEAPONS EXPORTS ASSISTANCE

The United States spends billions in a panoply of programs and agencies to support corporate commercial arms exports, according to the World Policy Institute's William Hartung. The Pentagon maintains a large bureaucracy devoted to promoting sales of military hardware by U.S. corporations to foreign governments. The Defense Department spends millions at military air shows to hawk the arms makers' wares, and it spends billions of dollars on loans, grants, credits, and cash payments to enable foreign governments to buy U.S. weapons.[74] Surely there are more efficient ways for the government to invest money if it is only concerned with creating jobs.[75]

Of course, weapons are not innocuous products, and there are severe costs to an arms exports policy driven by commercial impulses. Former Costa Rican President Oscar Arias has noted that the defense industry's weapons-pushing destabilizes countries and regions, as with respect to the removal of the ban on the sale of high-tech weapons to Latin America. The repeal of the ban was the direct result of industry lobbying. According to Arias, it "will certainly impede our efforts to break the vicious cycle of poverty and militarism."[76]

Commercial weapons exports may also undermine U.S. national security and humanitarian interests. As former Senator Mark Hatfield stated in 1995, "We can still enumerate dozens of cases where the transfer of U.S. military hardware has resulted in the misuse of those weapons, including human rights abuses and in the conduct of acts of aggression. Even more horrible is the fact that U.S. financed or provided arms have been used against our own soldiers in Haiti, Somalia, Panama, and Iraq."[77]

Why should the Pentagon subsidize commercial arms exports that may end up in the hands of dictators, may end upset regional stability, or which may be used against U.S. soldiers?

OTHER EXPORT ASSISTANCE AND OVERSEAS MARKETING PROMOTION PROGRAMS

Other government export programs have been the target of more sustained public and Congressional outrage, which has led to some partial but still inadequate reforms.

The Department of Agriculture's Market Access Program, once known as McNuggets for the World for its support of McDonald's advertising (when it was formerly the Market Promotion Program), is a $90-million-a-year program which is now limited to support of marketing efforts by farmer cooperatives and trade associations. The benign-sounding category of cooperatives, suggestive of small farmer arrangements, includes such operations as Sunkist and Ocean Spray, which are well able to afford their own advertising campaigns.[78]

Again, the Market Access Program and similar programs raise difficult questions: Why is export assistance a proper government function? Why does the market fail to provide incentives for advertising, lending, or other functions? And if businesses determine that a particular activity is not market-worthy, what *public interest* is served by the government filling the vacuum? If export assistance from other nations is the primary rationale for U.S. activities, how serious are efforts to negotiate an international agreement to curtail such programs? Finally, does the government receive an adequate return on its investment?

DEFENSE AND HIGHWAY PORK

It is important that "pork"—federal monies for unnecessary projects or inflated contracts—is understood as a subset of, not a synonym for, corporate welfare. While pork is a significant drain on the federal treasury, it is not, by and large, a helpful analytic term. Labeling a project "pork" stigmatizes it as unnecessary; the response of the project's defenders is to say that in fact the project is necessary. "Pork" does not offer objective criteria by which the dispute can be resolved.

Nonetheless, while analysts may differ over whether one or another project is pork, almost no one disputes that pork exists and is widespread. Pork is in part a reflection of our regional and state representative system of governance, with legislators trying to return federal dollars to their districts or states. But it is also derivative of a corrupt political system in which special interests exert an unhealthy influence.

PENTAGON PORK

The Pentagon budget is a bloated source of contractor pork. Without entering into a discussion of U.S. national security imperatives, it is clear from many official reports by both the Congress and the Executive Branch that much of what the Pentagon procures is unnecessary; that Pentagon waste and fraud is persistent; and that these problems reflect the political power of the military contractors.

One classic example of unnecessary procurement is the C-130 transport plane, which is built by Lockheed Martin in Georgia, near former Speaker Newt Gingrich's district and in the home state of former Senate Armed Services Committee Chairman Sam Nunn. The Air Force has requested just a small fraction of the more than 250 C-130 transport planes for which Congress has appropriated funds since 1978. The planes cost about $75 million apiece.[79]

Systematic corporate contractor fraud and waste have long been, and remain, too widespread at the Pentagon.[80] Among recent revelations, the Department of Defense Inspector General reported on spare parts provided to the Pentagon by Allied Signal at a 57 percent markup over commercial prices.[81]

It is important to understand the political underpinnings for ongoing Pentagon welfare and the failure to crack down on waste, because it illustrates the importance of competition and economic decentralization in curbing corporate welfare, and because it presents a case where outrageous corporate welfare benefits helped consolidate the political influence of narrow business interests.

During the early years of the Clinton presidency, the Pentagon encouraged the defense sector to consolidate, and it backed up its encouragement by subsidizing mergers through payments to cover the costs of consolidation —including extravagant "golden parachute" bonuses to executives of acquired companies. No industry knows how to respond to corporate welfare subsidies like the defense industry, in part because they conceive and lobby for them, as did Norman Augustine, the now retired CEO of Martin Marietta. The result of the Pentagon's encouragement is that military suppliers have undergone an ear-splitting consolidation that has left but three major prime contractors: Lockheed Martin, Boeing and Raytheon. Today's Lockheed Martin is the product of the merger of Lockheed, Martin Marietta, Loral, parts of General Dynamics and about two dozen other companies. Boeing leaped to the top tier of the contractor pack with its acquisition of McDonnell Douglas. Raytheon gobbled up Hughes.

With manufacturing facilities spread across the United States, these three companies now have enormous political influence—they can show that new military contracts will mean jobs in the districts of hundreds of Members of Congress, and in nearly every state. For districts where they do not have facilities, they can employ suppliers to help give them a political presence. This structural power, which is supplemented by major investments in campaign contributions and lobbyists,[82] helps enable the contractors to preserve the cycle of wasteful spending and abuse at the Pentagon. The tight consolidation of the industry also leaves the Pentagon much less able to deploy one of its most powerful sanctions against contractor wrongdoers—procurement disbarment—because of the paucity of alternative prime suppliers.

HIGHWAY PORK

The federal highway bills are another major source of pork. While important progress has been made in directing highway monies to road and bridge repair, as well as for modes of public transport, last year's highway bill, the Transportation Equity Act for the 21st Century (TEA-21) will allocate billions of dollars to new road construction, much of it unnecessary and harmful.[83] Instead of supporting modern mass transportation, Congress continues to surrender to the demands of road construction interests and the highway lobby. The harmful consequences include sprawl, air pollution and contributions to global warming.

LOANS AND LOAN GUARANTEES

As anyone who has been bombarded with credit card solicitations knows, there is no credit shortage in the United States. So why does the U.S. government enter into the business of making loans and issuing loan guarantees to large corporations? Corporations generally want loans from the government either because the loans are made at below-market rates, or because the loans include some sort of implicit subsidy (including de facto government insurance). This is a form of credit allocation that some legislators decry when applied to ordinary Americans.

Consider a loan recently approved by the World Bank, in which the United States is the largest country shareholder with an approximate 16 percent share. The $180 million loan package will help finance an oil pipeline that would transgress Chad and Cameroon, in Central Africa. The corporate beneficiaries of the loans include

Exxon and Chevron. The companies' consortium says that it plans to use the World Bank financing as the foundation for additional private financing. In other words, private lenders will be more willing to support the project knowing that the power of the World Bank stands behind demands for repayment. But if some of the world's largest oil companies do not feel comfortable financing an oil development scheme on their own, or if they are unable to attract private financing without government or multilateral lending agency support, perhaps that is a sign that the project should not go forward. (Critics point out that the project poses threats to rainforests, endangered gorilla-inhabited conservation areas and drinking water; and is likely to exacerbate ethnic conflicts with consequences potentially similar to those in Nigeria's Niger Delta or worse—political violence, some connected to prospective oil revenues, is already rife in Chad.[84])

Loans and loan guarantees are another corporate welfare category deserving a high degree of skepticism. For healthy companies, these kinds of government supports should be unnecessary. For cases where a political decision has been made that special circumstances merit some company or industry receiving loans or loan guarantees, Congress should adopt legislation that establishes a presumption of full repayment, at market rates. (For comment on bailout loans, see the remarks above.)

AGRICULTURAL SUBSIDIES

The government maintains a variety of agricultural subsidies, ranging from irrigation subsidies to crop insurance and price supports for certain commodities. Many of these benefits accrue to corporate agribusiness, and often support environmentally harmful farm practices (such as overuse of water). The original purpose of farm supports was to support family farmers and enhance stability in agricultural markets, and it is doubtful whether the programs still fill this function. At the same time, many farm supports were eliminated by the 1996 Farm Bill, with the general effect of promoting agribusiness consolidation and increased power for grain traders. Food prices have not declined. All of this suggests the need for a serious and open-minded reassessment of farm programs, so that the public interest in protecting family farms and sustainable agriculture is advanced, while subsidies for large agribusiness are curtailed.

CONCLUSION

Successfully ending corporate welfare as we know it will turn on a sustained campaign to educate, organize, and mobilize citizens. Merely documenting abuse is not sufficient to spark the national movement needed to trump corporate power. People need specific proposals to rally around, and a strategy which suggests our involvement.

With corporate welfare so pervasive at all levels of government, the campaign against it must be strategically savvy, multi-pronged and able to both create momentum and to take advantage of external events. After all, the looting of Uncle Sam is an ever-growing big business.

These are matters calling for creative thinking and approaches not only from legislators, but from law schools, political scientists, and economists. Unfortunately, a survey of law reviews and recent Ph.D. dissertations reveals a remarkable paucity of academic attention to the issue of corporate welfare; and until a June 1999 hearing of the House Budget Committee, there had never been a Congressional hearing devoted to a comprehensive assessment of the issue.

Here is an outline of proposals for discussion and reform. This list focuses on structural approaches, rather than itemizing programs that should be eliminated. The first set of proposals applies generally to corporate welfare, with the second being oriented around the categorization of corporate benefits outlined in this pamphlet. In the spirit of trying to spark a flexible, multi-pronged campaign against corporate welfare, some of the proposals overlap— different approaches may appeal to different people, and different proposals may fit different political moments. In the same spirit, these initiatives are intended to be provocative and are certainly open to criticism and refinement. Their purpose is to jumpstart creative thinking, debate, and mobilization for cutting corporate welfare.

ACROSS-THE-BOARD APPROACHES

A Bill to Eliminate All Corporate Welfare. A simple bill written to abolish corporate welfare could provide a valuable tool for citizen education and organizing. Such legislation would not propose a permanent ban on corporate welfare, which in any case would always be vulnerable to subsequent legislative action, but would require proponents of particular programs to mobilize support for the affirmative re-commencement of their favored subsidies under both procedural safeguards and reciprocal obligations. Then the advocates of the 1872 Mining Act could make their case for why such an abomination should be reinstated after elimination.

The central operative language for such a bill might read:

As of January 1, 2001, every federal agency shall terminate all below-market-rate sales, leasing, or rental arrangements with for-profit corporate beneficiaries, including of real and intangible property; shall cease making any below-market-rate loans or issuing any below-market-rate loan guarantees to corporations; shall terminate all export assistance or marketing promotion for corporations; shall cease providing any below-market-rate insurance; shall terminate all fossil fuel or nuclear power research and development efforts; shall eliminate all liability caps; and shall terminate any direct grant, below-market-value technology transfer, or subsidy of any kind to for-profit corporations.

As of January 1, 2001, the Internal Revenue Code is amended to eliminate all corporate tax expenditures listed in the President's annual budget.

As of January 1, 2001, the Internal Revenue Code is amended so that the value of local, county, and state tax subsidies to corporations shall be treated as income.

Where contractual arrangements or promises made in law preclude any action required by Sections (1), (2), or (3) without payment by the federal government to existing beneficiaries of programs to be eliminated, federal agencies shall take such actions as soon as possible without incurring such payment obligations.

Because of the complexity of the corporate welfare problem, such legislation would obviously need to incorporate considerable language amending existing laws. And even this approach would leave some corporate welfare problems unaddressed—such as the need to eliminate pork-laden or other programs in which the government should not be engaged, or for non-monetary commitments from corporations receiving government supports)—but it would be a very useful start.

Citizen Standing to Sue to Challenge Corporate Welfare Abuses. Citizens could be empowered to mount judicial challenges to runaway agencies that reach beyond their statutory powers. Taxpayers could be given standing to file such suits, by awarding a $1,000 "bounty" (plus reasonable attorneys' fees and court costs) for those who successfully challenge improper agency action. Consideration should be given to creating an incentive for such suits by awarding successful plaintiffs a percentage of the money saved through such suits, perhaps according to a sliding scale of declining percentage returns for higher savings and with a cap set at certain amount. Just as *qui tam* suits under the False Claims Act have helped curtail oil company underpayment of royalties owed the federal government, so such a measure would create a structural counterbalance to corporate influence over federal agencies.

Funding for Town Meetings. Small local, state or federal appropriations could fund dozens of town meetings across the country on corporate welfare and help educate the public.

Sunsetting Corporate Welfare. This would involve legislatures requiring that every program in which the government confers below-market-value benefits on corporations, including tax expenditures, automatically phases out in four years after initial adoption, and every five years thereafter. Under such a rule, the programs could of course be renewed, but only with affirmative Congressional or state or local legislative action. Sunsetting would overcome the problem of inertia by which both bad ideas and good ideas turned bad become entrenched corporate welfare programs protected from serious legislative review and challenge. The entrenchment problem is a particular problem for non-budgetary items, which are spared even the reviews accorded to appropriations.

Annual Agency Reports on Corporate Welfare. Every federal agency could be required to list every program under its purview which confers below-cost or below-market-rate goods, services or other benefits on corporations. They could also publish a list of every corporate beneficiary of those subsidies above a certain *de minimis* threshold, and the dollar amount of the subsidy conferred. This measure would spur much more news reporting on corporate welfare, and would generate public awareness by assigning proper names to the beneficiaries. Relevant state and local agencies could be required to make similar reports.

These reports should be published on the Internet, as should all other corporate welfare-related disclosures.

SEC Requirement for Corporate Welfare Disclosure. The Securities Exchange Act could be amended to require publicly traded corporations to list the subsidies (both by type and amount) they receive from governmental bodies, and to publish this information on the Internet. Alternatively, the SEC could mandate such disclosure through rule-making. This disclosure requirement is easily justifiable as in the public interest, since corporate beneficiaries are in many ways better positioned to report on the benefits they receive from government than the government conferrers. It would serve a valuable public purpose by assembling in a single location the dollar amounts of public subsidies accorded to the nation's largest corporations; and thereby enabling the citizenry to assess properly the extent and desirability of the subsidies. The disclosure requirement is also appropriate as a disclosure of material interest to shareholders. Government subsidies are of central importance to many of the nation's largest corporations, and to assess fully the value and future prospects of corporate earnings, shareholders have a right to information on government subsidies.

Limits on Executive Compensation in Government-Supported Corporations. Where the government is conferring substantial, voluntarily received benefits on corporations, it could reasonably limit the scope of beneficiaries to those who do not engage in particular sorts of socially undesirable behaviors. One such behavior is excessive executive compensation, which heightens income and wealth inequalities, and tears at the nation's social fabric. Government subsidies, including tax expenditures, could be denied to corporations whose executives receive more than a predetermined level of compensation, say those whose ratio of executive-to-lowest-paid-employee compensation is more than a certain amount, perhaps 30-to-1.

Prohibition of Government Subsidies to Criminal Corporations. The federal, state, and local governments take away fundamental rights, including the right to vote, from convicted felons who are persons. Corporations convicted of crimes rarely experience deprivations of anything near that scale. A small and appropriate step might be to deny any form of corporate welfare, including tax expenditures, to any corporation convicted of a certain number of felonies and/or misdemeanors. If the government is to confer subsidies on corporations, surely they should not go to enterprises convicted of criminal wrongdoing.

Reciprocal Obligations. The government should seek non-monetary reciprocal obligations from corporate welfare beneficiaries. These must necessarily vary by category of corporate welfare program and beneficiary. But two types of obligations are of special importance.

First is the requirement that certain subsidies be conditioned on beneficiaries enabling consumers to band together in non-partisan, non-profit, democratically governed organizations. This can be accomplished by allowing government-chartered consumer organizations that are accountable to their membership to include an insert, at no cost to the company, in the corporate welfare beneficiary's billing envelope, or publishing information on the company's web site. The insert would invite consumers to join the organization, which would work to contain prices, improve product quality and service, advocate for reforms, etc. This mechanism would be particularly appropriate for banks, thrifts and other lending institutions, insurance companies, HMOs, cable TV systems, and utilities.

Second, allocation of rights to government lands or other natural resources could be conditioned on beneficiaries agreeing to abide by environmental regulations, or even to uphold environmental standards that exceed those required by existing regulation.

LOCAL, COUNTY, AND STATE CORPORATE WELFARE

Where state and local authorities feel compelled to provide corporate welfare packages, they should consider inclusion of "clawback" provisions—mandating return of tax benefits if specific corporate promises are not kept —in agreements with corporate welfare beneficiaries.

Regional and National Compacts. Congressional legislation should authorize anti-corporate welfare compacts between states, enabling them to enter into binding arrangements to refuse to enter a race to the bottom against each other in terms of using special tax breaks and related benefits or stadiums to influence business, including sports-team, location decisions.

Surtax on Local and State Corporate Welfare. Congress should consider requiring the IRS to treat local and state corporate welfare expenditures as income upon which federal taxes should be paid.

GIVEAWAYS, INCLUDING R&D GIVEAWAYS

Prohibition on Government Giveaways. Government properties, whether real or intangible, should presumptively be sold, leased or rented to corporations for market rates. Although there may be exceptions (such as where consumer pricing considerations are considered of more importance than taxpayer reimbursement), there is generally no reason for taxpayer assets to be given away to corporations at less than market value.

Promote Competition in Allocating Government Resources. The market value of a government asset will vary based on the terms of the property transfer. Depending on the circumstance, taxpayer revenues may be lower if resources are allocated on a non-exclusive basis. But

there is an overriding broad public and consumer interest in promoting economic competition, and there
should be a presumption that, where possible, when taxpayer assets are to be transferred to corporations they be
conveyed on a non-exclusive basis.

Competitive Bidding. Especially where the government
plans to transfer taxpayer assets to corporations on an
exclusive basis, asset transfer prices should be established by auction.

Reasonable Pricing Provisions. Where there will be a consumer end-user from the transfer of government assets
(as in the case of products brought to market utilizing
government-controlled intellectual property rights), the
terms of the transfer should require the corporate beneficiary to agree to reasonable pricing provisions—a
requirement abandoned by the National Institutes of
Health in 1993. This is of primary importance for exclusive transfers, where transferees may gain monopoly
power. Because federal agencies, especially NIH, have his-
torically done a poor job in enforcing reasonable pricing
provisions, serious consideration needs to be given to how
such provisions should be administered and enforced.
Required disclosure of private investment in product
development, and correlating prices with amount and
proportion of private investment, may offer one fruitful
approach. It may also be possible to include reasonable
pricing guarantees in the bidding process, with preference
given to bidders making enforceable promises of lower
prices.

End Fossil Fuel and Nuclear Power R&D. There is no justification for federal support for these environmentally hazardous, nonrenewable energy sources. As study after study has demonstrated, energy efficiency and renewable energies represent future priorities.

INSURANCE, LOANS, AND BAILOUTS

No Discount Insurance. Consideration should be given to a legislative presumption against below-market insurance for corporations, requiring a special waiver for exceptions.

No Liability Caps. There should be a legislated blanket prohibition on liability caps, which unjustifiably protect corporations from paying for any harms they perpetrate. Liability caps, such as those in Price Anderson, should not accompany governmental insurance schemes.

No Discount Loans. Consideration should be given to a legislative presumption against below-market loans or loan guarantees for corporations, requiring a special waiver for exceptions, or perhaps a special waiver for corporations over a certain size.

Payback For Bailouts. Bailout beneficiaries should generally be required to pay back loans and outright bailouts in full, with interest, with priority given to repayments to the government over other claimants.

Preventing Foreseeable Financial Bailouts. H.R. 10 has lifted the regulatory walls between banks on the one hand and insurance and securities firms on the other, paving the way for the creation of too-big-to-fail financial holding companies, with federal deposit insurance likely to be de facto extended, at no charge, to other financial affiliates. H.R. 10 should be amended to include a provision establishing, in advance of imprudent risk-taking leading to future bailout demands, that no federal assistance will be made available to financial holding companies or to their non-bank affiliates. This provision will induce more prudent risk-taking.

CORPORATE TAX EXPENDITURES

Eliminate All Corporate Tax Expenditures. Because corporate tax expenditures are already compiled in the President's budget submission and by the Joint Committee on Taxation, this step would be less logistically complicated than ending all corporate welfare. Wiping the slate clean of corporate tax expenditures—perhaps the most deeply entrenched type of corporate welfare— would require the tax expenditure beneficiaries and their Congressional allies to justify anew these tax supports.

Require Reporting of Corporate Tax Expenditure Beneficiaries. The Internal Revenue Service should be required to publish a list of all corporate tax expenditure recipients over a certain *de minimis* level.

INDUSTRY PROMOTIONS AND EXPORT ASSISTANCE

End Government Market Promotion. Congress should prohibit government-run advertising and marketing schemes for private corporations.

End Export Assistance. Congress should eliminate export assistance programs, or making them available only on a strict means-tested basis.

Transcending liberal-conservative divisions, there is

a nascent national movement of consumer, taxpayer, environmentalist, labor, and small business groups that is waiting to be consolidated to stop corporate welfare. If these forces are united, they will form a powerful political force that can help rescue our political democracy from the narrow interests that now dominate it. Corporate welfare cuts to the core of political self-governance, because it is perpetuated in large measure through campaign contributions and the subversion of democracy; and because the continuation of corporate welfare itself misallocates public and private resources, generates unfair competition to companies not on welfare, and exacerbates the disparities and concentration of wealth, influence and power that run counter to a functioning political system in which the people should rule.

No chance, Ralph. There has NEVER been a "national movement" of any kind in this country.

NOTES

1 William Greider, *Who Will Tell the People? The Betrayal of American Democracy*, New York: Touchstone, 1992, p. 61.

2 Greider, p. 60

3 Paul Houston, "Influence of PAC Money on S&L Bailout Debated," *Los Angeles Times*, February 15, 1989, p.1

4 Edward Chadd, "Manifest Subsidy: How Congress Pays Industry—With Federal Tax Dollars—to Deplete and Destroy the Nation's Resources," *Common Cause Magazine*, Summer 1995, citing data from the U.S. Public Interest Research Group (PIRG).

5 See the Center for Responsive Politics' "Who Paid for this Election?" http://www.opensecrets.org/pubs/bigpicture/industries/05energy/bpindus05b.html

6 John Zebrowski and Jenna Ziman, "Tough Sell," *Mother Jones*, November/December 1998.

7 Lizette Alvarez, "Senate Repeals Tax Break for the Tobacco Industry," *The New York Times*, September 11, 1997, p. A26.

8 David Postman, "Stadium Opponents Unfazed by State Court—Special Election Upheld; Appeal Planned," *Seattle Times*, December 25, 1998, p. B5.

9 David Schaefer, "Allen Showed Them the Money—the Big Winners in the State's Most Expensive Campaign," *Seattle Times*, August 12, 1997, p. A1.)

10 Scott Stephens, "Schools in bad Shape, Study Says," *The Plain Dealer*, December 3, 1999, p. 1B.

11 Dean Starkman, "Condemnation is Used to Hand One Business Property of Another," *The Wall Street Journal*, December 2, 1998.

12 Scott Wilson, "Marriott Takes Deal to Stay in Maryland," *The Washington Post*, March 12, 1999.

13 Studies have concluded that many corporate location decisions are made on the basis of objective factors such as the labor pool, transportation, raw materials markets, schools, etc., and that the threat to move that elicits public subsidies is an added but not decisive windfall game that companies have perfected.

14 Jay Hancock, "Marriott Used Va. as Ruse to Raise Md. Bid; Public Records Suggest Bethesda Firm's Threat to Leave Was Bluff," *Baltimore Sun*, March 27, 1999.

15 See Joanna Cagan and Neil deMause, *Field of Schemes: How the Great Stadium Swindle Turns Public Money into Private Profit*, Monroe, Maine: Common Courage Press, 1998.

16 *Gambling on Trent Lott: The Casino Industry's Campaign Contributions Pay Off in Congress*, Washington, D.C.: Public Citizen, June 1999.

17 Paul More, Jessica Goodheart, Melanie Myers, David Runstein and Rachel Stolier, *Who Benefits From Economic Redevelopment in Los Angeles: An Evaluation of Commercial Redevelopment in the 1990s*, Los Angeles: The UCLA Center for Labor Research and Education and the Los Angeles Alliance for a New Economy, March 1999.

18 Peter Enrich, "Saving the States from Themselves: Commerce Clause Restraints on State Tax Incentives for Business," 110 *Harvard Law Review* 377 (1996).

19 Robert Pepper, Chief, FCC Office of Plans and Policy, letter to Senator Joseph Lieberman, September 6, 1995. The licenses are technically granted for eight years, but renewal is virtually automatic.

20 Bob Dole, "Giving Away the Airwaves," *The New York Times*, March 27, 1997.

21 Pepper, September 6, 1995.

22 For a description of how this could be achieved, see Ralph Nader and Claire Riley, "Oh, Say Can You See: A Broadcast Network for the Audience," 5 *Journal of Law and Politics* 1, (1988).

23 See People for Better TV, http://www.bettertv.org.

24 "Airwave Avarice" (editorial), *Los Angeles Times*, December 7, 1998.

25 For a history of passage of the 1872 Mining Act, see Carl Mayer and George Riley, *Public Domain, Private Dominion: A History of Public Mineral Policy in America*, San Francisco: Sierra Club Books, 1985.

26 Mayer and Riley, p. 79.

27 Michael Satchell, "The New Gold Rush," *U.S. News and World Report*, October 29, 1991.

28 Testimony of Stephen D'Esposito before the Senate Energy and Natural Resources Committee, April 28, 1998.

29 *Green Scissors '99: Cutting Wasteful and Environmentally Harmful Spending*, Washington, D.C: Friends of the Earth, Taxpayers for Common Sense and U.S Public Interest Research Group, 1999.

30 Thomas Power, *Not All That Glitters: An Evaluation of the Impact of Reform of the 1872 Mining Law on the Economy of the American West*, Washington, D.C.: Mineral Policy Center and the National Wildlife Federation, 1993.

31 D'Esposito, April 28, 1998.

32 "Investigation of Government Patent Practices and Policies: A Report of the Attorney General to the President," 1947, quoted in *Background Materials on Government Patent Policy: The Ownership of Inventions Resulting in Federally Funded Research and Development. Volume II: Reports of Committees, Commissions and Major Studies*, House Committee on Science and Technology, August 1976, p. 22.

33 For a fuller account of the taxol story, see Ralph Nader and James Love, Testimony Before the Senate Special Committee on Aging, February 24, 1993 (available at http://www.cptech.org/pharm/pryor.html).

34 See Nader and Love, February 24, 1993, especially Table 3 and Appendix A, for a close analysis of the federal involvement in discovery, pre-clinical research and clinical research of pharmaceuticals labeled as priority drugs by the Food and Drug Administration.

35 Heather Skale, "Gore's Efficient-Car Project Fuels Detractors; Environmentalists Fear It Will Run Dirtier," *The Washington Times*, June 26, 1999.

36 Complaint in *United States v. Automobile Manufacturers Association, et. al.* (1969), reprinted in Congressional Record, September 3, 1969 (91st Congress, 1st Session).

37 Tom Incantalupo, "Lean, Clean Driving Machine: Carmakers Switching Gears to Develop Green Cars," *Newsday*, March 8, 1998.

38 For a model legislation to create such an organization, see Robert Leflar and Martin Rogol, "Consumer Participation in the Regulation of Public Utilities: A Model Act," 13 *Harvard Journal of Legislation* 235 (1976).

39 See Ralph Nader and Jonathan Brown, *Report to U.S. Taxpayers on the Savings and Loan Crisis*, Washington, D.C.: BankWatch, February 1979.

40 *Glendale Federal Bank v. The United States*, 43 Fed. Cla. 390 (1999).

41 Stephen Labaton, "West Coast S&L Wins $909 Million from Government," *The New York Times*, April 9, 1999.

42 Labaton, April, 9, 1999.

43 See Laurence Kallen, *Corporate Welfare: The Mega Bankruptcies of the 80s and 90s*, New York: Lyle Stuart, 1991.

44 *Estaban Ortiz, et. al. v. Fibreboard Corporation, et. al.*, 1999 U.S. Lexis 4373 (1999).

45 "Analytical Perspectives," *Budget of the U.S. Government FY 2000*, Washington, D.C.: Government Printing Office, 1999.

46 Ibid., Table 5-2.

47 On the general matter of the anti-recycling bias of taxpayer subsidies, see *Welfare for Waste: How Federal Taxpayer Subsidies Waste Resources and Discourage Recycling*, Washington, D.C.: GrassRoots Recycling Network, Friends of the Earth, Taxpayers for Common Sense and Materials Efficiency Project, April 1999.

48 "Analytical Perspectives," Table 5-2.

49 For a compelling argument that tax expenditures frequently do not achieve their intended purpose in an efficient fashion, see Robert McIntyre, *Tax Expenditures—The Hidden Entitlements*, Washington, D.C.: Citizens for Tax Justice, May 1996.

50 "Analytical Perspectives," *Budget of the U.S. Government FY 2000*, Table 5-2.

51 *Foreign- and U.S.-Controlled Corporations That Did Not Pay U.S. Income Taxes, 1989-1995*, Washington, D.C.: General Accounting Office, March 1999

52 Robert McIntyre, *GAO Report: Big Foreign-Controlled Firms Operating in U.S. Pay Lower Taxes Than American Companies*, Washington, D.C.: Citizens for Tax Justice, April 1999.

53 To take one example of the earlier awareness, John LaFalce, D-New York, then chairman of the House Small Business Committee, and an array of expert witnesses at a February 1993 hearing described a peso meltdown to be a high probability almost two years before the crisis transpired.

54 Jill Dutt and John Berry, "In Rescue, Banks See Least Pain; Action Called 'Calming Force,'" *The Washington Post*, December 25, 1997.

55 "Asian Crisis: Impacts Worse Than Expected," United Nations Information Service, April 8, 1999.

    Similarly, the economic effects have been devastating in Africa, where the Fund has undertaken its traditional structural adjustment programs. Sub-Saharan African countries' debt burdens have risen under structural adjustment: African country debt rose 3.5 percent from 1997 to 1998, despite those countries paying $3.5 billion more in debt payments than they borrowed in 1998. The IMF took out nearly $1 billion more from Africa than it put in last year. The IMF's recessionary policies have led to stagnant economies; an internal IMF review found poor countries undergoing structural adjustment to have averaged zero percent growth from 1986 to 1996. Those outside of the program averaged 1 percent.

56 See Jay Solomon and Kate Linebaugh, "Indonesian Bank Merger May be the First of Many: IMF-Directed Move to Lift Capital Require-

ments Makes Deals Inevitable," *The Wall Street Journal*, January 20, 1998; Jeff Gerth and Richard Stevenson, "Poor Oversight Said to Imperil World Banking," *The New York Times*, December 22, 1997.

57 George Schultz, William Simon and Walter Wriston, "Who Needs the IMF?" *The Wall Street Journal*, February 3, 1998.

58 To see the full report, go to <http://phantom-x.gsia.cmu.edu/IFIAC/USMRPTDV.html>

59 In addition to the Price-Anderson Act discussed here, the industry benefits from government assistance in helping address its enormous waste problem, and utilities that own nuclear power plants are now seeking to unload the "stranded costs" of such facilities on unsuspected ratepayers as part of electricity deregulation. See Public Citizen's Critical Mass Energy Project, "Utility Deregulation: Why Should You Care?" available at http://www.citizen.org/cmep/ restructuring/utility.htm.

60 *The Price-Anderson Act - Crossing the Bridge to the Next Century: A Report to Congress, Division of Reactor Program Management*, Office of Nuclear Reactor Regulation, U.S. Nuclear Regulatory Commission, October 1998, (NUREG/CR-661).

As originally passed, Price-Anderson maintained a limit on operator liability, but did not maintain the industry risk sharing scheme. Until 1975, the Act limited liability for any single nuclear incident to $560 million. The unit operator was responsible for $60 million, and the federal government was responsible for the next $500 million. Following amendments and revisions in the program, the federal indemnity role has effectively ended.

61 Ibid., p.127

62 Ibid., pp. 127-128.

63 Ibid., p. 128.

64 Ibid., p. 128.

65 Ibid., p. 36.

66 Jeffrey Dubin and Geoffrey Rothwell, "Subsidy to Nuclear Power Through Price-Anderson Liability Limit," *Contemporary Policy Issues*, Vol. VIII, NO. 3, July 1990, p. 76. The subsidy calculation was based on the NRC's 1985 assumption that a worst case scenario accident had a .0000008 percent chance of occurring, and that such a worst case accident would cause property damage of no more than $10 billion.

67 Milton Benjamin, "NRC Issues Report, Withhold Worst-Case Estimates," *The Washington Post*, November 2, 1982.

68 *The Price-Anderson Act - Crossing the Bridge to the Next Century: A Report to Congress, Division of Reactor Program Management*, p. 128.

69 Congressional Budget Office, *Assessing the Public Costs and Benefits of Fannie Mae and Freddie Mae*, Washington, D.C.: Government Printing Office, May 1996, Summary Table 1.

70 Ibid.

71 Ibid.

72 Ibid., p. 35.

73 *The GSE Report*, Washington, D.C.: General Accounting Office, June 11, 1999.

74 William Hartung, *U.S. Weapons at War: United States Arms Deliveries to Regions of Conflict*, New York: World Policy Institute, May 1995. Hartung identified the Pentagon's Military Financing Program, the Defense Department's Excess Defense Articles program, the State Department's Economic Support Funds, the Export-Import Bank's "dual use" loan program and waivers of recoupment fees (designed to recoup payments to defense companies for R&D for domestic purposes) as among the arms export subsidy programs.

75 The jobs argument is further undermined by the fact that the U.S. arms exporters are increasingly pledging to foreign buyers that they will build their weapons in the purchasers' markets. These so-called "offsets" now amount to more than three-quarters of the value of U.S. arms sales, according to the Commerce Department, meaning that the economic benefits of the deals are being realized overseas, not in the United States. Hartung, *U.S. Weapons at War*.

76 Oscar Arias, "Stopping America's Most Lethal Export," *The New York Times*, June 23, 1999.

77 Senator Mark Hatfield, Statement to the Foreign Operations Subcommittee of the Senate Appropriations Committee, May 23, 1995.

78 See *Green Scissors '99: Cutting Wasteful and Environmentally Harmful Spending*, Washington, D.C: Friends of the Earth, Taxpayers for Common Sense and U.S Public Interest Research Group, 1999.

79 See William Hartung, *Military-Industrial Complex Revisited: How Weapons Manufacturers are Shaping U.S. Foreign and Military Policies*, Washington, D.C.: Interhemispheric Resource Center and Institute for Policy Studies, November 1998, available at http://www.foreignpolicy-infocus.org/papers/micr/index.html.

80 For a comprehensive review of fraud and waste, see A. Ernest Fitzgerald, *The Pentagonists: An Insider's View of Waste, Mismanagement and Fraud in Defense Spending*, Boston: Houghton Mifflin, 1989; and Andy Pasztor, *When the Pentagon Was for Sale: Inside America's Biggest Defense Scandal*, New York: Scribner, 1995.

81 Office of the Inspector General, Department of Defense, *Commercial Spare Parts Purchased on a Corporate Contract*, Washington, D.C.: Government Printing Office, January 1999. For other recent reports on fraud and abuse at the Pentagon, see "Pentagon's Fraud

Defenses Weak, Two GAO Reports Say," *The Washington Post*, September 29, 1998.

82 Defense contractors spent $8.5 million in the 1997-1998 electoral cycle on campaign contributions and nearly $50 million in 1997 on lobbyists, according to the Center for Responsive Politics. See http://www.opensecrets.org.

83 In their April 1999 report, *Road to Ruin*, Taxpayers for Common Sens and Friends of the Earth provide a list a roads projects they have found to be the most wasteful.

84 Korinna Horta, "The Exxon-Shell-ELF-World Bank Plans for Central Africa," *Multinational Monitor*, May 1997.

Friends of the Earth
1025 Vermont Ave. NW
Washington, DC 20005
(202) 783-7400
http://www.foe.org/greenscissors/

Taxpayers for Common Sense
651 Pennsylvania Ave., SE
Washington, DC 20003
(202) 546-8500 or Toll Free 1 (800) TAXPAYER
http://www.taxpayer.net

U.S. Public Interest Research Group (U.S. PIRG)
218 D Street, S.E.
Washington, DC 20003
(202) 546-9707
http://pirg.org/index.html

Project On Government Oversight
666 11th Street NW, Suite 500
Washington, DC 20001
(202) 347-1122
http://www.pogo.org

Consumer Project on Technology
P.O. Box 19367
Washington, DC 20036
(202) 387-8030
http://www.cptech.org

Essential Action
P.O. Box 19405
Washington, D.C. 20036
(202) 387-8030
http://www.essentialaction.org

Corporate Welfare Information Center
http://www.corporations.org/welfare/

The Benjamin Banneker Center
647 Plymouth Road
Baltimore, Maryland 21229
(410) 744-6293
http://www.progress.org/banneker/cw.html

Citizens for Tax Justice
1311 L Street NW
Washington, DC 20005
(202) 626-3780
http://www.ctj.org

Citizens for Leaders with Ethics and Accountability Now! (CLEAN)
1524 Tacoma Avenue South
Tacoma, Washington 98402-1806
(253) 572-1212
http://www.clean.org/welfare/welfare.html

People for Better TV
818 18th Street, NW, Suite 505
Washington, DC 20006
(888) 374-PBTV; (888) 374-7288
http://www.bettertv.org

Media Access Project
1707 L Street, NW, Washington, DC 20036
(202) 232-4300
http://www.mediaaccess.org

ICANN Watch
http://www.icannwatch.org/

Financial Markets Center
PO Box 334
Philomont, VA 20131 USA
(540) 338-7754
http://www.fmcenter.org/

50 Years Is Enough
1247 E Street, SE
Washington, DC 20003
(202) IMF-BANK
http://www.50years.org/

Center for Economic and Policy Research
1015 18th St., NW, Suite 200
Washington, DC 20036
(202) 293-5380
http://www.cepr.net

ACORN (National)
739 8th Street SE
Washington, DC 20003
(202) 547-2500
http://www.acorn.org

Center for Community Change
1000 Wisconsin Ave., NW
Washington, DC 20007
(202) 342-0567
http://www.communitychange.org/

Corporate Welfare and Foreign Policy
Janice Shields, Foreign Policy in Focus,
http://www.foreignpolicy-infocus.org/papers/cw/

Arms Trade Resource Center
World Policy Institute
New School University
65 Fifth Avenue, Suite 413
New York, NY 10003
(212) 229-5808
www.worldpolicy.org

Sierra Club
85 Second Street, Second Floor
San Francisco CA, 94105-3441
(415) 977-5500
http://www.sierraclub.org/

Union of Concerned Scientists
2 Brattle Square
Cambridge, MA 02238
(617) 547-5552
http://www.ucsusa.org/

Natural Resources Defense Council
40 West 20th Street
New York, NY 10011
(212) 727-2700
http;//www.nrdc.org

Critical Mass Energy and Environment Program
Public Citizen
215 Pennsylvania Avenue, SE
Washington, DC 20003
http://www.citizcn.org/cmep/index.html

Nuclear Control Institute
1000 Connecticut Avenue NW, Suite 804
Washington, DC, 20036, U.S.A.
(202) 822-8444
http://www.nci.org

Nuclear Information and Resource Service
1424 16th Street NW, #404
Washington, DC 20036
(202) 328-0002
http://www.nirs.org/

Physicians for Social Responsibility
1101 14th Street Northwest, Suite 700,
Washington, D.C. 20005
(202) 898-0150
www.psr.org

Public Citizen
1600 20th St. NW
Washington, DC 20009
(202) 588-1000
http://www.citizen.org/

Mineral Policy Center
1000 Connecticut Avenue NW, Suite 804
Washington, DC, 20036, U.S.A.
(202) 822-8444
http://www.mineralpolicy.org

Public Employees for Environmental Responsibility (PEER)
2001 S Street, NW, Suite 570
Washington, DC 20009
(202) 265-7337
www.peer.org

Forest Service Employees for Environmental Ethics
P.O. Box 11615
Eugene, OR 97440
(541) 484-2692
http://www.afseee.org/

American Lands Alliance
726 7th Street, SE,
Washington, D.C. 20003
(202) 547-9400
http://www.americanlands.org

Earthjustice Legal Defense Fund
180 Montgomery Street, Suite 1400
San Francisco, CA 94104-4209
(415) 627-6700
http://www.earthjustice.org

National Wildlife Federation
8925 Leesburg Pike
Vienna, VA 22184-0002
(800) 822-9919
http://www.nwf.org

American Rivers
1025 Vermont Ave., N.W. Suite 720
Washington, D.C. 20005
(202) 347-7550
http://www.americanrivers.org

National Audubon Society
700 Broadway
New York, NY 10003
(212) 979 3000
http://www.audubon.org

Citizens Against Government Waste
1301 Connecticut Avenue, NW, Suite 400
Washington, DC 20036
(202) 467-5300
http://www.govt-waste.org/
(conservative organization

ABOUT THE AUTHORS

RALPH NADER has co-founded numerous public interest groups including Public Citizen, Essential Information, Commercial Alert, the Center for Auto Safety, and the Center for Women's' Policy Studies. Green Party Presidential candidate for the year 2000, Ralph Nader continues to be a relentless force for grassroots activism and democratic change in the United States.

WINONA LADUKE is an Anishinaabekwe (Ojibwe) enrolled member of the Mississippi Band Anishinaabeg. She lives and works on the White Earth Reservation and is the mother of three children. As Program Director of the Honor the Earth Fund, she works on a national level to advocate, raise public support and create funding for frontline Native Environmental groups. She also works as Founding Director for White Earth Land Recovery Project; a reservation-based non-profit focused on land, cultural, and environmental issues. She is the 2000 Green Party candidate for vice-president, an author of two books and numerous articles and a graduate of Harvard and Antioch Universities.

ALSO AVAILABLE FROM THE OPEN MEDIA PAMPHLET SERIES

IT'S THE MEDIA, STUPID
John Nichols and Robert W. McChesney
Introductions by Barbara Ehrenreich, Ralph Nader, and Sen. Paul Wellstone

"With *It's the Media, Stupid* we move beyond a mere list of complaints about the commercial media system as it exists; we have an institutional analysis of the system that accounts for its hypercommercial and anti-democratic tendencies. John Nichols and Bob McChesney provide a careful description of the problem's various manifestations, and lay out a blueprint for media reform."
—JANINE JACKSON, Fairness and Accuracy in Reporting

"You hold in your hands a key to unlocking the corporate media chains that have shackled real freedom of the press and real democracy in this country for all too long. Use it!"
—RALPH NADER, from the introduction

$10.00 • 128 pages • ISBN 1-58322-029-1
TO ORDER CALL 1 (800) 596-7437
www.sevenstories.com

Corporations are picking our pockets.

Here's how to stop them.

SEVEN STORIES PRESS
140 Watts Street
New York, NY 10013
www.sevenstories.com

DISTRIBUTED TO THE U.S. BOOK
TRADE BY PUBLISHERS GROUP WEST

ISBN 1-58322-033-X

51000

9 781583 220337